Some of my Best
Friends are Blues

Some of my Best Friends are Blues

Ronnie Scott

With Mike Hennessey

Cartoons by Mel Calman

W. H. Allen · London
A Howard & Wyndham Company
1979

Filmset in 11/13 point Plantin
Printed and bound in Great Britain
by W & J Mackay Limited, Chatham
for the Publishers, W. H. Allen & Co. Ltd,
44 Hill Street, London W1X 8LB

ISBN 0 491 02239 5

To my partner, Pete King, without whom none of this would have happened . . . but don't worry, I'll get my own back.

R.S.

Acknowledgements

The authors would like to express their special thanks to Pete King for his invaluable help in supplying much of the material for this book. Grateful thanks are also due to Roy Burchell (*Melody Maker*), John Coldstream (*Daily Telegraph*), Ray Coleman (*Melody Maker*), Jeff Ellison, Benny Green, Johnny Griffin, Terry Henebery, Andy Hudson, Peter Jones, George Melly, Alun Morgan, Barry McRae, Spike Milligan, Jimmy Parsons and Stan Tracey.

Ronnie Scott and Mike Hennessey,
London, May 1979

Contents

Four Bars in . . .

Benny Green

The first time I ever heard Ronnie Scott mention the idea of a jazz club was in the bandroom of the Orchid Ballroom, Purley, in South London. The year was 1953. At the time, Scott, myself and seven others were waging a bitter, and in the end triumphant campaign to keep alive a co-operative orchestra whose strategy was to get itself booked into the dance halls, and then play uncompromising jazz once it got there. Already most of the country's bandleaders had conceived a deep loathing for us, which we did our best to aggravate on all possible occasions. The trouble was that an orchestra which splits the profits is a violent blasphemy against the dance band convention that the musician is a hired hand pledged to making the fortune of the band-leader, with whom he is expected to reach a relationship of grovelling servitude.

To the non-playing maestros of the period, our co-operative enterprise must have smacked strongly of syn-copated Marxism. If our little cell, starring Scott, proved to be the first of many, then the nation's bandleaders, threatened with redundancy, would have no choice but to go out and get an honest job. And yet, had our enemies been able to see us that night at Purley, they might well have tempered their distaste with a little sympathy.

The evening had been a disaster.

Scott and I were in the bandroom, slowly changing out

9

of our band uniforms and into what we laughingly called our street clothes and pondering the implications of the box-office returns. For the last five minutes we had been trying to work out how many times nine went into £14 6s 5d. Such mathematics was not good for the soul, so I was astonished when Scott remarked that he intended investing his share of the profits from our orchestra in a jazz club.

'What profits?' I asked.

'It won't always be like this,' he said. 'Not every date will turn out to be like this one.'

As it happened he was quite right. On the following Thursday we played at Acton Town Hall and were confronted with the depressing arithmetic of dividing nines into £12 10s 6d. It is therefore not really surprising that it took Scott another six years to realise his ambition.

Ronnie, as I remember him then, was possessed of an intense romanticism about jazz while, at the same time, having an utterly realistic approach to playing it. I think this apparent contradiction in his nature still exists and always resolves itself into a series of idealistic actions accompanied by a running barrage of his own sardonic self-criticism.

A natural straight-faced comic, Scott has always presented himself to audiences in an offhand, self-deprecating way and then proceeded to play as though his life depended on it, which in a way it does. An established jazz soloist while still in his teens, he has always indulged this tendency to carry the buffoonery right up to the moment when the music starts. But the true assessment of his achievements must be based not on the things he says, but on the things he does.

Even before the idea of opening his own club had

entered his head, he had for a long time shown a talent for organisation inside the chaotic world of modern jazz. As early as 1949 he had been a dominant influence in the formation of the country's first modern jazz club, the Club Eleven, and had later led a series of groups, ranging in size from a quartet to a full orchestra with varying degrees of success. This gift for marshalling the resources of others into some kind of ordered unity was less a question of administrative capacity than force of personality. It is one of Scott's most valuable assets and undoubtedly has a great deal to do with the success of many of his ventures.

A born night creature (he claims he can't begin to distinguish shapes until after 2 pm) Scott was naturally one of the musicians who frequented 39 Gerrard Street in both its near-beer and cabman's refuge phases. On his visits there he must have made a mental note that this could be one of several possible sites for the jazz club he still intended to open one day, though it was by no means the first choice.

In order to appreciate the magnitude of the task Scott was setting himself, one has to understand the state of the modern jazz club world during the late 1950s. Saturday night business was usually good. Sundays moderate, and the rest of the week more or less non-existent. All the known facts suggested that modern jazz in London was essentially a weekend affair, patronised by a tiny nucleus of loyal followers who were not prepared to turn out during the working week. And a more serious problem to be faced was the pitiful shoestring economy on which all jazz clubs were based.

Scott, however, had always been convinced that his dream of a salubrious and viable modern jazz club could become a reality. Throughout the penny-pinching era, he

11

himself had been the biggest local attraction in many of the London clubs—a factor which convinced him that a new potential audience was available to jazz musicians if only clubs adopted something approaching a night club policy. When Scott finally went ahead and opened the club in Gerrard Street, with a provisional policy of presenting British jazz four nights a week, the general reaction was typical of the dismally parochial thinking of the British jazz world in general. Nobody took the project seriously enough to assume it would last more than a few weeks. Musicians applauded and wondered how long it would be before the restless Scott moved on to some other dream scheme. My own reactions were typical enough. Like most musicians who had worked with Scott over the years, I had a healthy regard for his initiative, but it was not enough to convince me that he could ever come remotely near to achieving his aim of a high-budget club importing Americans. Scott was to open his club in the autumn. I felt that if he was still operating on New Year's Eve, he would be doing better than he could have hoped.

But, in fact, two years later Zoot Sims, one of the outstanding jazz figures of the last two decades, was playing a four-week engagement at the Club—and Scott had fulfilled one of his primary ambitions.

The early years of the Club were dominated by American saxophone players. This was due to something very much more than a personal whim on the part of the proprietor. Since the advent of the illustrious Coleman Hawkins in the late twenties, the saxophone had become the primary weapon in the jazz armoury. The so-called modern jazz of the fifties was produced almost exclusively by small groups consisting of one or two front line instruments and a rhythm section. Because so many of the major innovators and great musicians in jazz were saxophone players, it was natural that the instrument should have such pre-eminence. Thus it was no accident that many of the American instrumentalists who sprang automatically to mind as potential crowd-pleasers happened to play the same instrument as Ronnie Scott.

Scott's Last Expedition, of course, was the new club, opened in Frith Street on 17 December, 1965. It was obvious from the moment one stepped inside the door that the atmosphere had changed. Customers, especially the musicians among them, were immediately concerned about whether the musical policy would change, too. Whether or not this suspicion sounds cynical, it was justified by the surface evidence. It is one of the inscrutable economic laws of jazz clubs that as they become plusher, roomier and generally more sophisticated, so the music becomes increasingly adulterated and commercialised. Real, uncompromising jazz continues to reside principally in dingy basements with naked light bulbs and peeling paintwork.

With the move to Frith Street, Scott had increased his overheads enormously, with a small army of waitresses, barmaids, doormen and ushers. In order to make ends meet, he would have to attract at least twice as many customers as in Gerrard Street. Very often the only way to double attendance is to compromise the integrity of the music. This fear that in attempting to improve itself, London's one authentic jazz centre might in the process destroy itself, proved in the end to be unfounded—and the booking of alto saxophonist Lee Konitz was just one example of the way in which Scott brought the jazz historians as well as the floating fans running to the Club. And by booking the Buddy Rich band in April 1967, Scott

13

maintained his reputation for thinking up impractical ideas and making them work. By the time the Rich orchestra was booked in, members had been trained to expect anything.

If Scott had announced that Buddy Bolden was to give a recital at the Club, half of the members would have come along in good faith. And Ronnie was not above exploiting this unquestioning faith on occasions. More than once he announced a 'brief appearance by Toulouse Lautrec,' after which he would lower the microphone to the appropriate height and then leave the stand. There were always two or three customers who craned forward in expectation of the promised miracle.

Right through the 1960s, Scott was faced with a tricky problem in professional morality—to play safe and book the established masters, or reflect the changes and give an airing to some of the violent and elaborately perverse representatives of the jazz avant garde. Scott did both, booking Bud Freeman one minute and Ornette Coleman the next. The engagement of musical satirists like the Scaffold and Cheech and Chong provide further examples of the way he tried to broaden the commercial appeal of the Club without compromising its artistic values.

He has always believed that jazz can be made attractive to listen to if only it is presented in the right environment and in the right way. He has has never stopped insisting that good music is good music whatever it is called. He argues that the customer who has the patience and ambition to plumb the depths of a complex musician like Bill Evans will also be able to appreciate the muscial artistry of a classical guitarist, such as John Williams.

As for laughter, he has always maintained that it has a place in the jazz environment. If he had his way, which is his way of saying if he had a larger budget, the music would be sandwiched between recitals by stand-up comedians. As all frequenters of the Club know, he has done what he could to compensate, by becoming a comedian himself. If he could sing and dance, he would do that, too.

In his thirty-five years in jazz, Ronnie Scott has undoubtedly always occupied a unique position, especially with fellow musicians who learned a long time ago that he has a curious knack of making life more interesting for those around him. The success of Ronnie Scott's Club over the last two decades is a great tribute to his flair for making things happen—and making them happen with style.

Interlude 1

That was an intro by my good friend Benny Green. He'd like to have written more but unfortunately that's all the words he knows. Thank you, Benny.

Later in the book we'll be presenting Zoot Sims, Sonny Rollins, Ben Webster, Oscar Peterson, Dizzy Gillespie, the massed bands of the RAF, the Luton Girls Choir, the Red Arrows, the Bolshoi Ballet, the Moscow State Circus . . . and Miles. Sir Bernard Miles. He may not play as well as Miles Davis, but he always turns up on time; and he's a Sir, and everything.

What a galaxy of talent!

You don't seem very impressed. Why don't you all join hands and see if you can contact the living?

Actually, you should have been at the Club last Monday. Somebody should have been here last Monday. We had the bouncers chucking them in. A guy rang up to ask what time the show started and we said, 'What time can you get here?' The band was playing 'Tea For One' and at the end of the number the audience was on its foot. It was two hours before we found out our cashier was dead. Mind you, twenty years ago, when we first opened the Club, a dead cashier wouldn't have presented any problems. . . .

First Set:

Who's earning a living?

When Pete King and I decided to open a jazz club in 1959 we took heart from the fact that we were starting with two significant advantages. First of all, we knew that we couldn't lose much money in the venture because we didn't have any. And secondly, we didn't know that running a jazz club was impossible. In the early days people would say to us, 'Surely there must be easier ways of earning a living?' And we would, of course, reply: 'Who's earning a living?' It's sometimes hard to believe, looking around the Club today, that it had such humble beginnings and that there were times in the early days when things were going so badly that we had to sell clothes pegs to gypsies to keep in business. When Pete and I look back on twenty years of trial and error, of guesswork and gambling, bluff and blunder and all shades of luck from appalling to lousy, we can only wonder at how we ever had the cheek and temerity to plunge headlong into what has been described as a surefire recipe for financial disaster and mental breakdown.

With the distorting perspective of hindsight there is a danger of forgetting that when we first opened the doors of the basement at 39 Gerrard Street in Soho, we hadn't the remotest intention of building the Club into a major international jazz venue. The growth and development of the place was somehow forced upon us over the years; the

Club seemed to need to grow and we were sort of dragged along in its wake. The title of entrepreneur sits uneasily upon my ever-widening brow and I don't think Pete would claim to be one of nature's financial wizards. But the one constant in the twenty-year history of the Club has been our concern to provide good musicians with a decent place to play and jazz enthusiasts with a congenial environment in which to hear good music. We are very happy to have been able to do just that continuously since 1959, though I must admit that there have been times when the future looked as if it had been summarily cancelled.

After thirty-five years as a professional musician—a calling which is commonly held to turn even the most affable and benevolent of men into bitter cynics—I still feel a sense of wonder when I see great jazzmen who were the idols of my youth playing in the Club. It is an experience all the more potent for me because when I was a teenager the possibility of hearing American jazz musicians playing anywhere—let alone in the intimate atmosphere of a small club—was virtually non-existent. During the war there were occasional bottle party sessions when American musicians, on leave from the forces, would come and sit in with the resident British bands. But in the immediate post-war years, because of Musicians' Union restrictions, British jazz fans had absolutely no chance of hearing American jazzmen in person. One exception I do remember was a 'Jazz At The Philharmonic' charity concert in aid of the Flood Relief Fund which was held at the Gaumont State, Kilburn, in 1952 with giants like Oscar Peterson and Lester Young. That concert was something of an oasis for Britain's jazz enthusiasts and it may well have been on that memorable occasion that a seed of an idea was sewn in mind. Certainly all the musicians of my

18

generation who were happy to pay outrageous prices for 78 rpm records of Dizzy Gillespie and Charlie Parker were deeply frustrated about the restrictions that prevented their idols from appearing in Britain. But if anyone had told me in 1952 that one day such illustrious musicians as Dizzy Gillespie, Oscar Peterson, Count Basie, Woody Herman and Charles Mingus would be appearing in my own club, I would have said he was talking through his beret.

Until the restrictions on the employment of foreign musicians were lifted in the mid-fifties, jazz fans in Britain had to content themselves with listening to the home-grown product. But opportunities to hear our own up-and-coming modern jazzmen weren't exactly abundant. The fifties was the era of the boom in traditional jazz, and modern jazz was really the Cinderella music of the period. There was an all-out war between the mouldy figs and the modernists that was to be echoed years later in the pop world with the conflict between the mods and the rockers. At that time the trad bands were drawing all the crowds, and the beboppers reacted to public indifference by taking refuge in a kind of haughty elitism. Some of the more extreme among them sported goatee beards and wore sunglasses continuously to show their musical allegiance.

But the trouble with being a haughty elitist is that it is not only impossible to make a living, but it is also extremely difficult to find somewhere where you can be musically elite in public. Britain's modern jazzmen, in order to stay alive, had to compromise by playing in dance bands where flattened fifths were totally outlawed. But when they had time off they couldn't wait to find a handy broom cupboard or disused coal cellar where they could run through their precious Charlie Parker and Dizzy Gillespie licks and busk choruses on the magic chord sequence of 'How High The Moon'. I'm sure it was this irrepressible enthusiasm on the part of London's emerging modern jazz fraternity that sustained our Club in the early years when we never knew, from one week to the next, whether we would be able to keep going. Without that groundswell of enthusiasm, without that fund of goodwill and encouragement, I think we might well have shut up shop early on and diverted our creative energies to some much less daunting project like opening an English take-away in Gerrard Street.

Pete and I are gratified—and a bit amazed—that we've been able to keep the Club going for twenty years. It's a source of great satisfaction to us—and it really hasn't been that much of a struggle, considering it in retrospect. I suppose it would make a much more epic story if I could talk about fighting against overwhelming odds and desperate economic adversity—but it wouldn't really be true. Of course, we've had problems, but there has always been someone to come to the rescue when the future of the Club seemed in jeopardy and I am convinced that if the Club is widely regarded today as something of a jazz institution, it is because there have always been enough people—staff, musicians and jazz enthusiasts—who wanted to see the place prosper and develop. If Ronnie Scott's Club in 1979 is—as I've seen it described on a number of occasions—the world's finest jazz club, then it is because that's what all the people who have been involved or concerned with the venture, at some time or another over these last two decades, wanted to make it.

When Pete King gave an interview not so long ago about the history of the Club, he said, 'How we've achieved it, I don't really know. But one thing I do know—I'm bloody proud of Ronnie Scott's Club.'

Between you and me, I'm a little bit proud of it myself.

Interlude 2

I was born in a room over a Jewish pub in the East End of London called the Kosher Horses. Ours was a very poor family and my father was always out of work. He was a shepherd. But my parents used to go around the house all day singing the blues. Used to drive me crazy. Then one day I heard Mantovani—and I said to myself, 'That's my music—these are my people.'

Actually I'm not a Jew. Just Jewish. And Jewish people have very strong bonds of affection for one another. But my Uncle Ruben and his wife were constantly at each other's throats. I remember my aunt saying to Ruben after a particularly violent argument, 'What would you do if you came home from work one day and found me in bed with another man?' And my uncle said, 'I'd kick his guide dog.'

it's my son, the musician..

Second Set:

My son, the musician

What, you may ask, induced a carefree, happy-go-lucky, easy-going guy like myself to get involved in running a jazz club? After all, I'm the kind of person who gets worried when I don't have anything to worry about. Well, the standard answer to this question has always been that I started the Club so that I could guarantee myself somewhere to play—and it's absolutely true. If I hadn't been a musician, there would have been no Ronnie Scott's Club. However, the possibility of my being anything else *but* a musician never really occurred to me. I took up the trade because, at the time, it seemed a lot better than working, and I didn't feel I was cut out to be a neuro-physiologist, High Court judge, palaeontologist—or any of the other hand-to-mouth professions that my East End mates seemed to be drifting into in the forties.

My father was a musician—a very good saxophone player who worked under the name of Jock Scott and who was highly regarded in the profession—but that really wasn't a factor in my becoming a musician because my mother divorced my father when I was about four. I really have no childhood memories of my father and, of course, he wasn't around either to encourage or discourage me when I decided I wanted to be a musician.

I was born on 28 January, 1927 in one of those typical little East End terraced houses in Aldgate. The rooms were tiny, there was a boiler in the kitchen and we had a postage-stamp backyard. We were a poor family but I never remember wanting for anything and the house was always spotless. My father was from a Russian immigrant family and my mother's ancestry was a mixture of Portuguese and Dutch. I was brought up by my mother and my grandmother. My mother used to work at the Houndsditch Warehouse Company and eventually she got married again to a man who worked for the same company. Then we made the usual Jewish trek from the East End to Stoke Newington, then to Stamford Hill and finally to Edgware. Unaccountably, we missed out Golders Green.

The first musical instrument I ever owned was a cornet which I bought for five bob in a junk shop on the way to school. I was rather proud of it, even though it was completely unplayable. It took me a little time to realise that the valves were supposed to spring up again when you released them after pushing them down. I soon gave up the cornet and bought myself a soprano saxophone. I believe it must have been the original prototype soprano saxophone, as invented by Sir Charles Soprano. It had a double octave key, several pads missing and a hideously mangled reed. Of course, I didn't know anything about reeds then. But I managed to get some noise out of the instrument, which sounded like a severely constipated hyena. And when my mother heard me play a few faltering bars of some tune or other she was as proud and delighted as only a good Jewish mother can be. It was definitely a case of 'My son, the musician'—and she soon persuaded my stepfather to buy me a tenor saxophone.

I took saxophone lessons from Vera Lynn's father-in-law, Jack Lewis (that's still one of my principal claims to fame) and long before I had any kind of competence on the instrument, I was playing semi-pro gigs with a bunch of local musicians whose collective nerve and enthusiasm left their talent a long way behind. When we couldn't con people into hiring us to play at their weddings or barmitzvahs, we used to hang around places where real musicians played. There was something awe-inspiring and irresistibly exciting about the dance band world of the forties and I was desperately eager to get into a band uniform, climb behind a music desk and wait for my turn to stand up and take a booting tenor solo. When I say I was desperately eager, I mean that I couldn't even wait long enough to master the barest rudiments of playing the saxophone.

One of the most active, jazz-orientated bandleaders of the time was drummer Carlo Krahmer who'd been playing professionally since 1936. He worked in the bands of Johnnie Claes, Claude Bampton and George Shearing and between 1943 and 1950 he was resident at the Feldman Swing Club, the forerunner of today's 100 Club in Oxford Street, and also worked at the Nuthouse Club in Regent Street. In 1947 Carlo founded the great Esquire Record label and worked hard for the cause of jazz right up to his death in April 1976.

When I first came into contact with Carlo, he was running the band at the Jamboree, a bottle party club in Wardour Street which was later to become the Flamingo. I was one of a clique of young musicians who used to frequent the Jamboree and hang around the bandstand breathing in the heady atmosphere of the glamorous life of the professional musician. If the band played 'Honeysuckle Rose' or 'Lady Be Good'—one of the half-dozen tunes we could play with swaggering inexactitude—then we were sometimes allowed to sit in.

I had just about six months of lessons from Jack Lewis in Stamford Hill and had been playing about a year when Carlo, clearly a man with a discerning ear for burgeoning talent, asked me join the band. It was something of a unique offer as band jobs go. First of all it was a little on the short-term side—two weeks to be precise—and secondly, a condition of my engagement was that I didn't actually *play* the saxophone. The fact was that Krahmer's tenor player, Len Wood, was leaving the band and his replacement—Jimmy Skidmore—couldn't start for a fortnight.

'Would you like the gig?' Carlo asked.

'I'd love it—but my playing really isn't up to it,' I said.

'No problem,' Carlo replied. 'I'm contracted to present a six-piece band here so all you have to do is sit on the stand and go through the motions for two weeks.'

And that's exactly what I did. I tossed off a few notes here and there just to reassure myself, but for most of the time I might just as well have been a cardboard cut-out.

Most nights a lot of musicians would come into the Club and sit in. I remember the fine Belgian trumpet player, Johnnie Claes, was one of them and there were other good musicians on leave from the Air Force or the Army, like Ronnie Chamberlain, Geoff Gough and Louis Stephenson—all excellent saxophone players. The young musicians I'd been hanging around with continued to come to the club and when we had a guest star on the stand, I'd sit with them at one of the tables and just listen. That was my first professional gig. It really wasn't the most demanding job I've had, but it was a great experience.

After that I went back to the semi-professional life of youth club and wedding gigs, fighting a constant battle to sneak some jazz tunes in between the 'Palais Glide' and the 'Hokey Cokey'. There were two principal 'labour exchanges' for musicians in those days—the *Melody Maker*, where bands used to advertise for musicians and musicians used to advertise for gigs, and Archer Street, an unprepossessing thoroughfare off Great Windmill Street at the back of Piccadilly Circus where musicians would congregate every Monday in search of work.

The 'Engagements Wanted' column of the *Melody Maker* was the battleground for a frantic contest to have the first ad in the appropriate section and it was consistently won by an 'Able Accordionist' from Ilford. In its editorial columns the paper used to carry items about personnel changes in the various bands of the day—and these sometimes heralded the possibility of a resident gig. For example when the trumpet player in Alf Goldberg's Romany Apache Band at the Golden Paradise Club got fired for knocking off the girl singer and cutting out Alf, you'd see a paragraph in the *MM* which would run:

'Nat Simpkins, lead trumpet player with the Alf Goldberg band at the plush Golden Paradise niterie, is leaving the residency to concentrate on his extensive freelance gig connections.'

Well, it happened that the tenor saxophone player at a West Indian bottle party club in New Compton Street called the Bouillabaisse, decided to concentrate on his extensive freelance gig connections—and I took his place. The bandleader was Clarry Wears; Tony Crombie was the drummer; and the trumpet player was Ronnie Fenner. The owner of the club was a West Indian called Bah whose most impressive characteristic was that he had had half of one ear bitten off in a fight. I can't remember too much about the gig itself, but I do remember that I was over the

26

moon to be working as a full-time professional musician. It was every bit as exhilarating and stimulating as it had always seemed from the other side of the bandstand. I really felt that I had now arrived as a fully-fledged West End musician. It could only be a matter of time before my name would feature in a *Melody Maker* paragraph, even if the Wears band didn't run to a 'femme thrush'.

One of the leading tenor saxophone players of that era was Reggie Dare, a man who accompanied his playing with positively epic flourishes of the shoulders and who always managed to *look* as if he was playing superbly even when he was coasting. I was a dedicated 'Reggiedarian', not only because of his elaborate choreography and his sumptuous, breathy ballad style, but also because he worked with a quartet—just himself and a rhythm section—and I thought that was the perfect and proper showcase for a tenor saxophone star. It was the kind of set-up that was a feature of the American jazz scene, but there were not too many groups of that kind working in London in the forties.

Reggie was sharing a double residency with a band run by Johnnie Claes. They worked alternate sets at two restaurants which backed on to each other—the Potomac in Piccadilly and the Princes in Jermyn Street. Johnnie was looking for a tenor player—I think Johnny Gray was leaving—and I managed to get an audition. I struggled through it without too many fluffs and it was arranged that I should sit in with Johnny Gray that night at the Potomac for one set so that I could learn the ropes. I've never been a great reader and I really produced some spine-chilling goofs. They gave me a chance to busk my way out of trouble on 'My Blue Heaven'—but by this time my nerves were shattered. Afterwards Johnnie said, 'Son, you sound very good and you busk OK, but we really want somebody who can read.' Actually I was unimpressive both as a reader and a busker—but Johnnie was very kind.

I must have brushed up my playing a little bit after that because six months later Johnnie Claes took his band on the road and hired me. It was a marvellous experience. Johnnie was a very forward-looking bandleader and the band was really good. Dennis Rose was on trumpet and the drummer was a little black guy called Freddie Crump who must have been all of fifty years old. He had the worst drum kit in the world—nobody else could have played it. He'd painted a pattern of black diamonds on the bass drum shell which was hopelessly out of true and his cymbals were about half an inch thick, but he played fantastically well. He did an act in which he drummed on everything in sight—his teeth, people's coat buttons, glasses and bottles . . . everything. I suppose it was easier than playing that kit. There were a lot of laughs in that band.

I was with Johnny for about eighteen months; then in 1946 I joined the Ted Heath Band—and that was *really* the big time because Ted's band boasted some of the finest musicians in the country—Kenny Baker, Alan Franks and Stan Roderick on trumpets; Johnny Gray, Reg Owen, Les Gilbert and Dave Shand on saxophones; Jack Bentley and Harry Roche on trombones; Norman Stenfalt on piano; Charlie Short on bass; and Jack Parnell on drums. It was an excellent band and, to be honest, I was a bit out of my depth in that company. Still, it took me a full nine months to get fired. Jack Parnell was planning to form his own band and he asked me if I'd be interested in joining him. I said I would—and later, when Ted came to me when we were playing at the Hammersmith Palais and asked me if I was going to join Jack's band, I, like an idiot, said, 'Yes'. That was a tactical error which was compounded after we played a gig in Liverpool. When it was over all the other guys in the band went back to London on the night train because we had a West End engagement the next day. But I was still intoxicated by the heady experience of being a big time musician—so I decided to book into a top hotel and fly back in the morning. That night Liverpool had its worst snowstorm in twenty years—and the next day, by the time all possibility of a flight back had been ruled out, it was too late to catch a train to make the gig. I think Tommy Whittle was brought in to dep for me and a few days later I received a letter from Ted Heath saying that my services were no longer required.

I did eventually join Jack Parnell's new band, but not until 1951. I've often wondered since what might have happened if I'd kept my job with the Heath band—because it certainly wasn't the sort of band a musician would normally choose to leave. Had I stayed I might have been a different kind of musician entirely and I might never have gone into the jazz club business.

Interlude 3

It was harebrained of me to have taken a chance on air travel in the depth of winter. After all, as I've often reflected since, if God had meant us to fly, he would have given us all El Al tickets.

I remember once flying with my band to a gig in Stockton and as we were approaching the runway, the pilot came on the intercom and said, 'We're about to land in Stockton—please set your watches back a hundred years'.

Not many people know this, but they dropped an atom bomb on Stockton. It did £15 worth of damage.

Actually I spent a wonderful fortnight there one Sunday. We stayed at one of the cheaper boarding houses—the sort of place where you have to wipe your feet on the way out. I remember the rooms were very small—you turned the doorknob and it rearranged the furniture

But the landlady was a nice old girl. She was Irish. Typically Irish—she had a green face. She used to do the cooking and pygmies came all the way from Africa just to dip their arrows in her soup.

It was the only place I've stayed where the seagulls used to bring the guests bits of bread.

I remember the landlady said a funny thing to me when I arrived:

'I hope you have a good memory for faces.'

'Why?' I asked.

'Because there's no shaving mirror in the bathroom.'

A bit later on I saw the landlady and told her I wanted to talk to her about the ceiling in my room.

'What about it?' she asked.

'I'd like one.'

I'm pretty certain there was a ceiling in the Greenwich Village hotel I stayed in when I made my first trip to the States in 1947—but I couldn't be sure because I spent most of the time making the rounds of the jazz clubs. . . .

Third Set:

Geraldo's navy

The musicians of my generation suffered a major frustration in the late forties and the fifties because, short of raising the substantial amount of cash needed to make a return trip to the United States, they were denied the opportunity of hearing their great modern jazz idols—except through the medium of the few 78 rpm records which were more or less inadvertently released by the record companies. American musicians just couldn't get permits to play in Britian even if there had been any promoter or impresario who was prepared to invest in modern jazz concerts.

So in 1947 Tony Crombie and I decided that if the mountain was not about to come to Mohammed, it certainly wasn't going to budge an inch for a couple of young Jewish boys. We resolved to blue all our available funds on a jazz holiday in New York. We reckoned that as we were in a desperate hurry to get there but in no hurry at all to get back, we'd make the outward journey by air and come back by sea.

Well, *we* may have been in a hurry—but Icelandic Airways adopted a more leisurely approach and the trip to New York, via Shannon, Reykjavik and Gander, took us twenty-two hours. But we didn't really care because every minute of the journey was taking us nearer to the fabulous jazz centre of the world. We had the address of a very inexpensive hotel in Greenwich Village and, as soon as we arrived, we dumped our bags and set off for legendary 52nd Street. It was on this street, in the forties and fifties, that the new jazz which had sprung from the uptown clubs like Minton's Playhouse and Monroe's was developed and elaborated. On 52nd Street, between Fifth and Sixth Avenues, were half a dozen clubs where great jazzmen, including the illustrious pioneers of the bebop movement, used to play—clubs like the Three Deuces, the Famous Door and Jimmy Ryan's.

We went straight to the Three Deuces and we caught the Charlie Ventura band featuring trombonist Bill Harris. It was a fantastic experience for us because we'd never really heard an American group in a club before—just a few musicians from the bands of Glenn Miller and Sam Donahue during the war.

We hung out in New York for a couple weeks, taking in all the clubs. We had open tickets for the boat trip back but we didn't even think about returning until we were down to our last few dollars. Our style of living was not exactly extravagant and we were able to make our meagre funds last a bit longer by calling on my Uncle Phil for dinner one night. Uncle Phil was a tailor but he seemed to make more money as a punter, because he spent most of the evening telling us how much money he'd won on the horses. As a betting man myself, I was full of admiration—and rather reassured that if we did find ourselves stranded in New York, Uncle Phil was in an incomparably good position to help us out.

I think we had about 25 dollars between us when we decided it was time to book our return passage. We went to the Cunard Office and found to our dismay that the first boat we could get on was not due to sail for ten days. Even in those days 25 dollars didn't go an awful long way in New York. We cut down our food consumption to two coffees and a shared doughnut per day and presented ourselves at the Cunard office every morning in the hope that there might be available space on an earlier boat. And when things got fairly desperate, I put our last-resort plan into action. We went to see Uncle Phil.

'Listen, Uncle Phil, Tony and I are absolutely skint and we can't get a boat for some days. Would you help us out and lend us 100 dollars? We'll send it back to you as soon as we get home.'

I'll say this for Uncle Phil—he didn't hesitate for a moment. 'No,' he said.

Happily, the following morning we were told that we could get on the *Ernie Pyle*, a converted corvette, which was leaving in two days. It carried 300 passengers, had a self-service cafeteria and instead of individual cabins, male and female dormitories. But we didn't care—we were high on American music and I remember I was still exulting in the tremendous impression that the Three Deuces had made on me. The idea of presenting modern jazz in that intimate kind of atmosphere kept recurring in my mind with accelerating frequency. I had plenty of time to reflect on it, too, because the voyage home took nine days.

Ironically enough, my next major engagement as a musician was on the maiden voyage of the newly refitted *Queen Mary* in a band led by drummer Bobby Kevin. If only I'd known that I would be going on the boats, and not only travelling to New York in style but getting paid for it as well, I would certainly have saved myself the upheaval of that under-financed earlier trip. Bobby had a good band—with Johnny Dankworth on alto, Tommy Pollard on vibraphone and Ken Moule on piano. Leon Calvert was supposed to be the trumpet player but just before we sailed he developed appendicitis and we had to settle for a 65-year-old who may not have been the best trumpet player in the world, but was certainly the worst. That rather spoiled things for us musically, but there were substantial compensations. In those days the musicians really had the run of the boat and it was a great life. When we got to New York there was the customary maiden voyage fire float and hooter welcome—then it was off to the hotel and straight on to the jazz club circuit.

New York was a fabulous contrast to the austerity of post-war London and most of the musicians tended to indulge in a little light smuggling. Tommy Pollard used to bring back model aeroplane engines; Peter Ind, the bass player in the First Class band, used to concentrate on shirts. American shirts and ties in those days were hugely coveted by the more hip British musicians. Peter used to buy the cheapest shirts he could find and sell them in England at a healthy profit. He'd take the new shirts out of their wrappings and put them in with his soiled linen to get them through Customs. One evening, two hours before the *Queen Mary* was due to sail, he came on board smiling the wide smile of a man who has pulled off an immense coup. He'd apparently found a place in the Bronx that was selling off overstocks of brand new shirts at about 5 dollars a dozen—or some such trifling amount. Peter bought two dozen and was enthusiastically contemplating a profit margin of some 900% as he began unpacking them. He unwrapped the first one—and observed with some chagrin that it only had one sleeve. So did the second. And the third. In fact, the twenty-four shirts had only twelve sleeves between them.

'Looks like the sleeves have been ripped off, as well,' I said to him. 'You'll have to sell them to Wingy Manone,' What he said to me was not really fit for a young tenor player's ears.

I did a few trips on the *Mary*, in 1948, playing fairly boring dance music in the cabin class ballroom; but we ratings, in what became known as Geraldo's navy—since Geraldo booked the bands for the boats—lived well and there was always the bonus of being able to listen to the great jazz names in the New York clubs. We'd usually arrive in New York in the morning and leave the evening of the following day—which gave us a full night to do the jazz rounds. I'll never forget the night I heard the quintet of the great Charlie Parker with Miles Davis at the Three Deuces. And playing next door, incredibly, was Dizzy Gillespie's Big Band. Miles later sat in with Dizzy's outfit. It was a really memorable night.

My next engagement was with the band of accordionist Tito Burns which I joined in October 1947. We were on the road for a while and played a summer season in exotic Cliftonville. Tony Crombie was in the band, with Pete Chilver on guitar, Dennis Rose on trumpet and Terry Devon, who later married Tito, was the singer. There were a couple of night club jobs as well—I was in the Jack Nathan Band at the Coconut Grove (which we naturally used to call the Coconut Grave) and in a band co-led by Jack Jackson and Hamish Menzies at Churchill's. Jack and Hamish would get a little overtired sometimes and while Hamish would be calling for 'Tea For Two', Jack would be counting us into 'Dinah'. But most of the time it seemed to work out. I also worked for a while for Ambrose, who'd always been a great idol of mine. He put together an all-star band for a lavish new night club called the Nightingale (would you believe, in Berkeley Square). It must have been one of the most expensive bands of all time. It included Kenny Baker, Harry Hayes, Charlie Short, Harry Roche, Norman Stenfalt and three singers. I can't remember now whether or not the story is apocryphal, but it is said that a guest at the club once sent up a request to Ambrose wrapped in a £5·00 note—and Ambrose sent the request and the fiver back, wrapped in a £10·00 note.

Even in the best of bands, the professional life of a musician represented a constant artistic compromise because the music that we had to play in order to live wasn't the music we lived to play. So the incorrigible jazzmen among us would congregate whenever the opportunity arose and play unadulterated, unrelenting jazz. To make this easier, a group of us got together in January 1949 and rented a rehearsal room at 41 Great Windmill Street, which we ran co-operatively as the Club Eleven. There were ten musicians—Leon Calvert, Hank Shaw, Lennie Bush, Joe Muddel, Bernie Fenton, Tommy Pollard, Tony Crombie, Laurie Morgan, Johnny Rogers and myself—and a manager; hence the Club Eleven.

Our doorman at one time was a huge black boxer called Charlie Brown who had the bizarre distinction of being the landlord of 10, Rillington Place in Notting Hill—the house in which mass murderer John Reginald Halliday Christie lived. The Club Eleven soon became known as a Mecca—if you'll pardon the expression—for modern jazz fans, and we had many memorable sessions down there.

Ever since leaving Ted Heath I had been waiting for Jack Parnell to get his band under way but his plans seemed to have got off to a grinding halt. So when Jock Scott, my father, offered me a job in his band on the

Caronia, which was leaving on a world cruise in December 1949, I decided to accept it. It was the only occasion I ever worked with my father and I must admit it wasn't too exciting because Pete Blannin, the bassist, and I were the only young guys in the band. The other musicians were amiable enough, but of a different generation. The boat sailed from Southampton to New York, then we did two ten day cruises to the West Indies and returned to New York. The *Caronia* was then scheduled to head back to 'Southampton the fields', way via the Pacific Ocean. But by this time I'd had enough and wanted to get back home. I was heavily involved with a young lady at the time and had no enthusiasm at all for the prospect of spending another couple of months at sea. When we got to New York the *Queen Mary* was in dock and was due to sail back to Southampton the next day. So I buttonholed Ray Feather, the tenor player in one of the *Queen Mary* bands, and persuaded him that he'd like nothing better than a round-the-world cruise. Then I called my mother and got her to send me a telegram saying that my grandmother was very ill and I should return home immediately. I took the telegram to the purser on the *Caronia* and after much protestation and turmoil, Ray and I were allowed to swap gigs. My father, needless to say, was severely disapproving of the whole squalid deception.

I got back to England on 17 January 1950, and I went down to the Club Eleven and played like Charlie Parker, Lester Young, Don Byas, Dexter Gordon, Lucky Thompson and Coleman Hawkins all rolled into one. But since then I've given up smoking the stuff.

Interlude 4

Although the Club Eleven could get pretty smoky and sweaty, it had so much more atmosphere than some of the dance gigs we had to play. I remember we did a date once at a place right out in the sticks where it was so quiet they had to shoot an old man to start a cemetery.

If more than three people stood together they thought it was a riot.

The night life there finished in the afternoon.

I asked a cab driver where all the action was and he took me to this place where they were fishing illegally.

It was so dull up there—they had one set of traffic lights in the whole town. They changed once a week. People used to come out and watch. It was the kind of town where you plugged in your electric toothbrush—and the street lights dimmed.

We got so bored having nothing to do that we used to sit in the band bus and mix LSD with chopped liver and take trips to Israel. Actually it was a combination of dubious substances that was to put the Club Eleven out of business in the spring of 1950. . . .

Dont ask—
I was fired from
Geraldo's navy—
I got seasick on
the Boat Train..

Fourth Set:

The joints were jumping

In April 1950 the Club Eleven moved from Great Windmill Street to 50, Carnaby Street. Nobody had ever heard of Carnaby Street at that time and it was innocent of tourist-trap shops, photographers with monkeys and over-lit, white-tiled bathrooms selling green icecream. But that was nevertheless the time when the Street really was swinging. Not quite in the 52nd Street class, though almost as drab and featureless—on the outside.

With the change of premises we decided to adopt a change of policy and start presenting top American acts. We wanted to inaugurate the new policy in a fairly spectacular way so we carefully compiled a letter to Billie Holiday, making her an offer we were convinced she couldn't refuse. We said we would pay her a full 250 dollars for a week at the Club and would graciously provide her with hotel accommodation. Although none of us in the Club Eleven was particularly devoted to the vocal art, we knew that Billie Holliday, the first lady of jazz would have great public appeal. It would be a great coup to have her. For reasons either of total inexperience in booking major foreign artists or, more probably, of economy, we neglected to mention the inconsequential matter of the return transatlantic air fare. One further flaw in the arrangements was that we didn't have an address for Billie Holiday, so we sent the letter to her care of the American jazz magazine, *Down Beat*. You may not believe this, but we never did get a reply.

So the new policy was short-lived. And so, as it happened, was the new Club Eleven.

On the night of 15 April 1950, I was on stage with my band, eyes tightly closed, blowing the last of nine choruses of Charlie Parker's 'Now's The Time'. The Club was packed; the joint, as Fats Waller used to say, was jumping. I finished my solo, opened my eyes and got the shock of my life. A massive uniformed police sergeant practically filled my entire field of vision. I backed up, looked around and saw that the place was full of coppers. Commotion, confusion, consternation.

'All right—stop the music and turn out your pockets,' barked the sergeant.

The music stopped abruptly and the ensuing near-silence was only broken by the sound of little packets hitting the floor. We were being raided by the drug squad—and the joints were jumping. Those of us in the band had no time to unload the evidence and we were among a dozen guys who were rounded up by the police and transported by black Maria to Savile Row police station. We were all pretty naïve, apprentice potheads but the police seemed to be even more uninitiated in matters relating to *cannabis sativa* than we were. One of the musicians used to make a hole in a matchbox, put a joint in the hole and then slightly open the box and use it like a pipe. When the desk sergeant at Savile Row took possession of this rude accessory he announced to one of his colleagues with pontifical assurance: 'Yes, there you are, you see—they sniff the stuff through that hole.'

We all spent the night in the cells and I suppose we ought to have been terrified—but we were altogether too artless and unworldly. I remember one of the musicians crawling on his hands and knees to the door of the cell and doing the Château d'Yf bit with hoarse cries of 'Water! Water!' The next day we appeared at Marlborough Street magistrates' court all charged with offences under the Raw Opium Regulations and the Dangerous Drugs Act. And of course, the newspapers, in their usual enlightened and objective way, were full of implications and innuendoes about 'drug-crazed beboppers'.

The court case was pure Beachcomber. The Chief Inspector who led the raid said that there had been 250 people in the Club when the police entered. 'The Club is a bebop club run by musicians who recently moved from other premises in Soho,' he explained.

Then it happened. The magistrate actually, shamelessly, flagrantly, manifestly, overtly and unreservedly said it. 'What,' he asked solemnly, 'is bebop?'

For us in the dock, for whom bebop was something of a musical religion, providing a definition would have represented a fairly daunting challenge. But Chief Inspectors learn to take these summary queries in their stride:

'A queer form of modern dancing—a Negro jive,' he answered with brisk authority.

He then went on to reveal that the police had found on the floor of the Club a couple of dozen packets of hemp and one of prepared opium.

We were remanded for a week and all but one of the twelve charged were found guilty. The magistrate then summed up before announcing the penalties.

'We are dealing,' he said, 'with young people of tremendous force of character and great vitality. They are intelligent . . .' Thus far it was the best reference I'd ever had in my life. But after that it deteriorated sharply:

41

'. . . and, of course, they are in a stage of their existence when they repeat and copy what is done by other people. The social effect of this matter is not confined to these young people before me by any means, and that is why it is important that every step should be taken to completely squash this drug business right from the very beginning without any hesitation and quite ruthlessly. That is what I propose to do. This is a very serious case.'

I swear at that point that I could hear eleven hearts plummeting into eleven sets of boots. I felt the blood drain from my head and I couldn't seem to focus my eyes properly. Penal servitude? Deportation? Salt mines? Chain gang? I tried to brace myself for the exemplary, punitive sentence. Then, I listened with a mixture of disbelief and intense relief as the magistrate handed out fines ranging between £5·00 and £15·00.

In retrospect the story seems hugely innocent and trivial—but if I seem to be flippant about that particular escapade, it is not because I don't deplore the use of hard drugs—however limited it may be. I have strong feelings on this subject, especially as I have seen narcotics destroy the lives of one or two very close friends.

The Club Eleven folded very soon after that episode and apart from a brief club venture in the basement of the Mapleton Hotel in 1953, in association with the Flamingo Club, I didn't involve myself in the jazz club business again until October 1959 when we opened the Club at 39 Gerrard Street.

It was early in 1951 that Jack Parnell's much-deferred plans to form his own big band finally came to fruition when he was persuaded to put an orchestra together for a new musical show. It was in that band that I renewed the acquaintance of Pete King whom I'd first met in the late forties when he was a member of a semi-professional band, led by Jack Oliver, which used to play at Stoke Newington Town Hall. I would play one-night stands there occasionally with Tito Burns's Band. Pete, a fellow tenor player, had followed me into the Vic Lewis Orchestra—and then in April 1951 we found ourselves in the saxophone section of the Jack Parnell Band. Our first major engagement was to provide the music for 'Fancy Free', a twice-nightly show at the Prince of Wales Theatre starring Tommy Trinder and Pat Kirkwood. The band included Bob Burns, Derek Humble, Dave Shand, Harry Roche, Don Lusher, Jimmy Watson, Max Harris, Sammy Stokes and Phil Seamen. We didn't work in the orchestra pit but on a dais at the right-hand side of the stage. Jack Parnell used to stand almost on the stage to conduct with the rhythm section up front, followed by the strings, then the saxophones, then the brass section. It was a fine band, but after you've played exactly the same music twice-nightly, six nights a week, for a couple of months, it becomes increasingly difficult to sustain interest in the musical proceedings. Musicians in those circumstances are constantly seeking distractions and, in that band, most of the distractions were provided by trumpeter Jimmy Watson. There was a pub opposite the stage door and Jimmy had worked out the places in the score where he had sufficient bars rest to enable him to slip off the stand, hurry to the pub, down a pint and get back on to the stand in time for his next cue. Whenever he was missing, the saxophone section used to take bets on whether or not he'd miss his cue—but in the six months or so that the show ran, he never failed to get back in time.

Occasionally, when there were breaks in the music for a ten-minute sketch, Jimmy would forego his pint, slip off

43

his chair, crawl through the saxophones and the violins, come up behind Max Harris, who'd be sitting at the piano chewing his nails or just dreaming, and bite him very sharply in the calf. We'd see Max's face contorted in agony, the pain of the bite being rendered more exquisite by the frustration of his having to keep silent.

As the months wore on, the band became more and more unruly and the saxophone section became an artillery line of paper pellet shooters with the long-suffering Max Harris as the invariable target. I remember misfiring once and hitting Tommy Trinder full on his celebrated chin as he was coming offstage. There was a big row about that and Jack had to speak to us all very sharply. None of us in the band was inconsolable when the show folded in November. Jack reorganised the outfit adding Jimmy Deuchar and Ken Wray and went out on the road.

I didn't stay with the band for very long—I think there was probably a girl involved and I wanted to get back to town for a while. Jack had difficulty getting broadcasts for the band because the BBC regarded it as primarily a jazz outfit. So to render the band a little more commercial, he decided to hire a girl singer. The singer he chose happened to have a husband who played tenor saxophone and she would only agree to join the band if her old man was also given a job. So to make way for the new man, Jack fired Pete King—and in so doing tore the heart out of the band. Because when they heard the circumstances of Pete's dismissal, a lot of the guys quit—among them Jimmy Deuchar, Derek Humble and Ken Wray.

We were all sitting in the Harmony Inn in Archer Street one day in January 1953 when we conceived the idea of forming a nine-piece co-operative band—and it turned out to be one of the better ideas we had that year. Derek

44

Humble, Benny Green, Pete King and myself were on saxophones, Jimmy Deuchar on trumpet, Ken Wray on trombone, Norman Stenfalt on piano, Lennie Bush on bass and Tony Crombie on drums. And we had a singer called Johnny Grant. We were managed by Harold Davison, an impresario who has always had a soft spot for jazz and to whom the Frith Street Club owes a substantial financial and moral debt, and our public début was in Manchester in February 1953. We had a month of bookings in the Manchester area and from the very first night the band really took off. In April we played the London Palladium as part of one of Ted Heath's Sunday Swing sessions and I remember the headline over the review in the following week's *Melody Maker* was: 'Scott punches Heath fans at the Palladium'. It was meant to indicate that the band played with a lot of punch—but then ambiguous headlines are not unknown in the *MM*.

Art Baxter joined the band as vocalist in August. He was a good singer but something of an acquired taste as a performer. He had a kind of surrealistic approach to stage presentation and if the audience didn't respond to him with due acclaim he'd shout out as he walked off stage, 'Aw, f. . . you!' I remember we had a gig in Cheltenham once and Art missed the band bus. We were just about to hit the stage when he arrived at the stage door and said, 'Hey, Ronnie, can you give me the fare for the taxi?'

'Yeah,' I said, "How much?"

"£15.00,' Art replied. He'd made the whole trip from London by cab—and £15.00 was half a week's wages in 1953.

The band went from strength to strength and got good reactions everywhere. It was not only good musically, but we were very commercially minded and concerned with

45

good presentation. We had marvellous music stands in pale blue plexiglass with a v-shaped base and a white scroll desk and each man had his name inscribed on the scroll. The stands were lit from behind so that the plexiglass glowed impressively. We wore blue uniforms with check waistcoats and we really looked terrific on stage.

One first band bus was a bit primitive and to keep warm in winter we carried an oil heater the intricate technology of which no one but Lennie Bush was able to master. If Lennie arrived late, we froze.

So we had a good band, great desks and uniforms, a good library, a full engagement book, a fair bus and an unfair oil heater. All we needed now was a gimmick. We decided to buy a monkey, dress it in its own made-to-measure band uniform and take it on stage with us as a kind of mascot. That was one of the worst ideas we had that year. We bought the monkey but as soon as we took it on the bus it went berserk. It was terrified and nobody could get near it without running the risk of having several fingers bitten off. Its behaviour was so erratic that some-one was moved to observe that it had probably had a man on its back.

The band had a few personnel changes during its life. Victor Feldman replaced Norman Stenfalt and we'd feature Victor in a drum duet with Tony Crombie that always brought the house down. Then Tony left and was suc-ceeded by Phil Seamen, and Henry Shaw took over on trumpet from Jimmy Deuchar.

The nine-piece lasted about two-and-a-half years and then, inevitably, it broke up. Inevitably because all bands have an optimum life and it is rarely more than three years. Added to which there were so many stars in that band that clashes of temperament became more and more frequent.

But it was tremendous fun—and very satisfying musically. I've never laughed so much in my life as I did with that band.

It is part of the mysterious alchemy of tour organisation that it you have a gig in Canterbury one night, the following evening you have to be in Perth, and Exeter always immediately precedes Aberdeen. On those all-night bus journeys some of the conversations were hilarious, full of that oblique, sardonic, black and blue humour for which musicians have a unique reputation. For example, we used to make-up ideal names for various categories of people—there was Mustapha Fix, the Turkish tenor player, Pete Bog, the Irish flautist, Mannheim Stoned the German trumpet player and the famous Indian jazz critic Pandit Unmer Sifflee—later to figure in one of the club's *Melody Maker* ads.

If the monkey mascot was the worst idea we had in 1953, the lousiest idea of 1955 was the one I had to form a big band. To run a big jazz band you have to be obscenely rich and quite insane—so I went into the venture only half qualified. It took hardly any time for me to see that the project was a disaster, but it took almost a year to make a practical acknowledgement of the fact by folding the band. There were some fine musicians involved—Douggie Robinson, Joe Harriott, Pete King and myself on saxophones; Stan Palmer, Hank Shaw, Dave Usden and Jimmy Watson on trumpets; Jack Botterill, Robin Kaye, Mac Minshull and Ken Wray on trombones; Norman Stenfalt on piano; a Swiss musician called Erik Peter on bass; and Phil Seamen on drums. But it was a case of the whole being considerably smaller than the sum of the parts—or maybe that some of the parts were full of holes.

After the death of the big band I co-led a band with Tony Crombie for a while. We made a ten-inch LP for Decca in February 1956 and I remember that it contained Stan Tracey's first recorded arrangement—'It Might As Well Be Spring'. Also in this period Pete King and I staged one or two jazz evenings at a place called Fordham's at 39 Gerrard Street—an address with which we were later to become much more intimately connected.

In February 1957 I took a sextet to the United States as part of one of the first Anglo-American band exchanges. Britain got Eddie Condon's All Stars and America got Jimmy Deuchar, Stan Tracey, Lennie Bush, Allan Ganley, Derek Humble and myself. It should have been Phil Seamen on drums, but he was detained at Southampton before boarding the *Queen Elizabeth* and charged with possession of certain illicit tablets. We tried everything to get the authorities to let Phil make the trip and deal with the matter on his return. We phoned the local magistrate but we couldn't seem to get across to him how vital it was for Anglo-American relations for Phil to be on the tour. In the end we had to call Harold Davison from the *Queen Elizabeth* and get him to fly out Allan Ganley.

We had been, quite incongruously, booked to tour with an all-black rock 'n' roll package that included Fats Domino, Chuck Berry, La Vern Baker and Bill Doggett. They needed a British bebop band like they need a synagogue in Damascus. In some places our names weren't even on the billing, but when they did appear, they just about outranked the printer in type size. We played our one number on each date to enormous and totally indifferent audiences and then got the hell off.

It was when I got back from that tour that I teamed up with Tubby Hayes to form what was generally acknowledged to be one of the best modern jazz groups Britain ever produced—the Jazz Couriers.

Tubby was twenty-two years old and he had already established himself as one of the most gifted, mature and technically accomplished musicians on the British jazz scene. He had been playing tenor saxophone since he was twelve and he invested everything he did with a terrific vitality and enthusiasm. He really made you *want* to play and I learned a tremendous amount from him. I remember our two and a half years together in the Jazz Couriers as one of the most satisfying and musically productive periods of my career.

The Couriers made their début on 7 April 1957 at the opening of the New Flamingo Club in Wardour Street and thereafter worked fairly steadily. In addition to Tubby and myself, the band featured Terry Shannon on piano and Bill Eyden (later Phil Seamen) on drums, and an assortment of bass players including Malcolm Cecil, Phil Bates, Jeff Clyne, Spike Heatley, Kenny Napper, Lennie Bush and Pete Blannin.

One of the highlights of the Couriers period was a two-week British tour with Sarah Vaughan. The band also made a few record dates and won a couple of polls. But, once again the Scott law of optimum durability came into play and by the summer of 1959, though nobody actually said as much, we all knew the Couriers were running out of steam and getting a little stale. So we decided to fold the band, and on 30 August, 1959, we played our last date—at the City Hall in Cork.

Interlude 5

I certainly had a lot of laughs on the road with various bands but some of the places we had to play were pretty unsalubrious.

I remember one town where the seagulls used to fly upside down. Nothing worth shitting on. And the locals are not exactly over-endowed with intelligence. When decimal currency came in they raised the school-leaving age to thirty-five. I'll give you an example of the mentality: I went into a chemist's shop up there and said to the guy behind the counter, 'Do you have cotton wool balls?' And he said, 'What do you think I am—a teddy bear?'

I understand that the only reason that Jesus wasn't born in that town was because they couldn't find three wise men. Or a virgin, for that matter. There was one woman up there who had triplets and her husband spent six months looking for the other two blokes.

Anyway, having been on the road on and off since the age of sixteen, I decided it was time to stay in London and get into the club business in a serious way. . . .

Fifth Set:

My chef, the gorilla

The basement at 39 Gerrard Street had been various things in its time—a bottle party rendezvous during the war years and a taxi-drivers' refuge and occasional jazz club venue when the bottle party era ended. It had a couple of billiard tables, a few chairs and a small counter where you could buy tea and sandwiches. Quite a few musicians used to use the place, either to hang out between gigs, or else to rehearse or play a jazz gig for a handful of fans. We knew Jack Fordham, who ran the place, pretty well. He had a number of properties around the West End but this particular venue, as I recall, was not helping to make him rich. It was what you might call a stopping concern. Jack knew that Pete and I had often talked about opening a club, so one day he approached us and asked if we would like to rent the place. Pete and I discussed it for about fourteen seconds and agreed. It was a simple as that—so it was more a matter of 39 Gerrard Street finding *us*, rather than our finding *it*.

The division of responsibilties between Pete and myself presented no problems because Pete had been business manager of both the nine-piece band and the big band. So the idea was that I would play at the Club on a fairly regular basis and Pete would count up the money—if any.

We borrowed about £1,000 from my stepfather, took a lease on the place, bought some secondhand furniture and a few pots of paint and, with the aid of some press-ganged volunteers, started doing the place up. We built a small bandstand, bought a small grand piano, moved out the billiard tables, cunningly converted the tea bar into a coffee bar—and we were in business. The place was somewhat Spartan—it didn't quite match up to the Three Deuces—but it was a start.

On Friday, 30 October, 1959 came the moment which I had been anticipating, off and on, ever since that night on 52nd Street in 1947 when I'd seen the Charlie Ventura 'Bop For The People' Band in full cry and marvelled at the electric atmosphere of the club. We launched Ronnie Scott's Club with a stentorian fanfare of publicity and a positive fusillade of advertising—a four-inch single column spot in the classified section of *Melody Maker*:

RONNIE SCOTT'S CLUB
39, Gerrard Street, W.1.
Fri. 7.30 pm Tubby Hayes Quartet; Eddie Thompson Trio and the first appearance in a jazz club since the relief of Mafeking by Jack Parnell.
Membership 10/- until January 1961. Admission 1/6 (members), 2/6 (non members.)

That was the first of a series of none-too-serious weekly advertisements which we hoped would grab a bit more attention that the usual kind of ad.

The opening night went well and I couldn't have chosen two better groups to inaugurate the Club than those of Tubby Hayes and Eddie Thompson. Tubby was to play many more times at the Club and also to figure in several UK-US band exchanges. He could hold his own with the best players in jazz and his death in June 1973 was a great personal blow and a tragic loss for music.

Eddie Thompson, of course, has been a major name in the realm of jazz piano for years. He has one of the sharpest musical wits in the business and, incidentally, an unmatched talent for tune title distortions like 'Don't Way That Be', 'Isn't This A Rainy Day To Be Loved In The Court', 'I Water The Front Cover' and 'I Don't Chance A Stand With A Ghost Like You'. There was a good attendance by some of London's top jazz musicians and I remember that a special visitor on opening night was Ray Nance, trumpet player, violinist and vocalist with the Duke Ellington band.

We were paying something like £10 a week to rent the premises. We met our running costs out of membership and entrance fees and whatever was left over we split among the musicians. For the first couple of years we were restricted to presenting British musicians because of the continuing difficulty of securing work permits and Musicians' Union permission for foreign instrumentalists. In that period most of Britain's leading modern jazz musicians appeared at the Club in various combinations—Joe Harriott, Ronnie Ross, Jimmy Deuchar, Johnny Dankworth, Dizzy Reece, Victor Feldman, Derek Humble, Ken Wray, Dick Morrissey, Harry Klein, Kenny Graham, the other Peter King, Pete Blannin, Rick Laird, Jackie Dougan, Phil Seamen, Lennie Bush, Tony Crombie, Kenny Napper, Malcolm Cecil, Jeff Clyne, Terry Shannon, Don Rendell, Harry South, Tony Kinsey, Gordon Beck, Ronnie Ball, Eddie Harvey, Ron Mathewson, Benny Green, Bill LeSage, Hank Shaw, Jimmy Skidmore, Bert Courtley, Kathy Stobart, Allan Ganley, Benny Goodman (the drummer) and, of course, Stan Tracey, who was house pianist at the Club for seven years.

Business was generally good right from the start. That

first weekend we had sessions on Friday, Saturday and Sunday evening. Later we started so-called 'all-nighters' on Fridays and Saturdays until 3 am. But although we got good crowds, both Pete and I soon recognised that we'd have to wait a while before retiring to palatial residences in the Bahamas. The problem was that we suddenly began to discover what a legion of friends we had among musicians—and, naturally, we couldn't ask our friends to pay admission charges when they dropped into the Club. We sometimes had more potential sitters-in in the audience than non-players because, as I indicated earlier, opportunities for modern jazzmen to play in congenial surroundings were only minimally more abundant than teetotal bass players.

Our sole publicity in those days was a poster on the railings outside the Club and a weekly advertisement in *Melody Maker*. I decided from the beginning to try to make the announcements humorous rather than solemn so that they would stand out a little bit from the other ads in the paper. I suppose I thought there might be a spin-off in that people would start looking for them each week. I don't know if the humour made any difference in real terms, but it gave some indication of the spirit and atmosphere of the Club.

This was the sort of thing we did:

'14 November, 1959: At tremendous expense and great loss of life—now open seven nights a week. Come along and see the fun next week—we're holding a musicians' ball.'

I remember that a full two weeks after accepting and printing that announcement, the *MM* sent me a very prim letter saying that they couldn't accept advertisements containing that kind of double entendre!

28 November, 1959: 'Saturday, midnight to 6 am—the late, late, late, late show. Now featuring a tremendous step towards inter-racial relations—ham beigels.'

5 December, 1959: 'Free admission!—for Sir Thomas Beecham, Somerset Maugham and Little Richard.'

12 December, 1959: 'Ronnie Scott's Club—sponsored by the Shoreditch Tsetse Fly Protection Society.'

And this was the week in which one of the most-remembered lines appeared:

'Food untouched by human hand—our chef is a gorilla.'

2 January, 1960—Special offer to our 1,000th client—a pair of exquisitely matched giant bird-eating spiders, or a week in Manchester. Personal appearance of Alfred Hinds.

Then another highly durable line:

'The food must be good—3,000 flies can't be wrong.'

(I actually looked that one up in the *MM* files just to check it and we really did have only 3,000 flies in 1960, not half a million as we have today. I must remember to order more Flit)

We tried hard to improve the amenities as we went along, but as money was tight, progress was necessarily leisurely. Slowly, however, the Club was building a reputation for good music and atmosphere. Visiting jazz people, when in town, would drop into the Club and, if we could persuade them, would sometimes sit in. Some of the early visitors were singer Donna Hightower; the Modern Jazz Quartet; arranger Manny Albam; Freddie Green, Snooky Young, Billy Mitchell and Thad Jones—all from the Basie band of 1960; and, from a touring Jazz At The Philharmonic package, Joe Gordon, Richie Kamuca and Shelly Manne. I'm pretty certain that it was Shelly's enthusiasm for the Club atmosphere that prompted him to

55

open his Manne Hole club in Hollywood in November 1960.

We were paying musicians something like £3 a session and a resident player like Stan Tracey would be earning about £35 for eight sessions a week. We paid our few members of staff £10 or £12 a week and I think the coffee bar was a kind of concession. Or, perhaps, more of an imposition. We had not yet the realms of high finance. The problem was—and still is, to a certain extent—that native musicians tend to be taken for granted, however brilliant they may be, so people did not exactly flock to Gerrard Street in their thousands. Furthermore, there was no room to dance—and people used to dance to jazz in those days; it was very much a key element in the so-called trad jazz boom. People liked to do 'that queer form of modern dancing—that Negro jive.'

We had a succession of cleaners who used to 'live in'—in other words, they slept at the club—and one of the more picturesque of these was a little guy called Arthur. Arthur had two principal convictions: one was that Guinness was so inestimably good for you that a consumption of one or two gallons per evening was an indispensable pre-requisite for a healthy life; the other was that the Club was a regular meeting place for Russian spies. Arthur would walk around the Club with two bottles of Guinness and a glass in his right hand and two more bottles in his left and, keeping a watchful eye open for any customers with traces of snow on their boots, would very quietly and unostentatiously get paralytic. Apart from these two preoccupations, Arthur was a good cleaner, and a most trustworthy employee. Like most of the people who have worked for us over the last twenty years, Arthur really cared about the Club and took pride in his work.

He'd been with us about six months when, one night, he telephoned Pete King at his home. It was just after four in the morning.

'Listen, Pete,' said Arthur plaintively, 'I just left the Club to get a breath of air and the police followed me back here and want to take me away. Can't you speak to them?'

Pete, still half asleep, muttered, 'What's this all about, Arthur?'

'I honestly don't know,' said Arthur in a state of considerable anguish.

'OK, then, put one of the policemen on the phone,' Pete yawned.

The copper came to the phone very reluctantly and explained that Arthur had been seen in Gerrard Street trying the door handles of parked cars. So Pete asked to speak to Arthur again.

'Is this true what the police say, Arthur?'

'Of course not, Pete,' said Arthur offended, 'You know me. It's all rubbish.'

The next day Arthur appeared in court and was remanded for a couple of weeks on bail. The case came up in Marylebone Magistrates' Court and Pete King went along to give a character reference. Pete explained to the court that Arthur had worked for us conscientiously and dependably for six months, had been a model of honesty, had never filched so much as a packet of crisps, nor a halfpenny from the till, and was generally a pillar of probity, a veritable monument of integrity. Pete left the witness box feeling like a combination of Perry Mason and Marshall Hall; he sat down at the side of the court and gave a cheerful nod of assurance towards Arthur in the dock.

Then a detective sergeant climbed into the witness box and proceeded to read out a list of Arthur's previous convictions which seemed to go on forever. It was a most varied and comprehensive catalogue of crime and, naturally, Pete was positively cringing with humiliation, his face a study in slack-jawed incredulity.

Yet in all the time he worked for us, Arthur really was a scrupulously honest and dedicated employee. It is one of the most rewarding aspects of the last two decades that the loyalty and dependability of the people who have worked for us has been quite exceptional. It seems to suggest that we've been doing one or two things right.

Arthur carried on working for us for a while but he had to give up sleeping at the Club—not because of his predilection for nocturnal perambulations but, as he explained to me, 'I'm getting fed up with this great bird that comes down every night after I've gone to bed.' And when he said 'bird' he wasn't referring to a girl—but to an eight-foot tall vulture or archeopteryx that he was convinced was terrorising him nightly. Come to think of it, it *could* have been a toucan. . . .

Things ticked over reasonably smoothly through 1960, but both Pete and I knew that if the Club were to survive we couldn't go on just marking time. We had to find ways of bringing in more paying customers and the logical catalyst for this was a liquor licence. Licensing laws were tougher then than they are today and in order to be able to serve alcohol, we had to become a *bone fide* club with rules and membership cards and a club committee. So we completed the necessary formalities and on 14 April, 1961 we got a licence entitling us to serve alcoholic drinks until 11 pm. Later that year we added a kitchen to the Club's amenities, put in a fire exit and successfully applied for a supper licence enabling us to serve liquor until 1 am. I'm sure we didn't comply strictly with the law—I don't think it would have been economically possible—but we behaved with as much civic responsibility as we could permit ourselves and, astonishingly enough, in the six years of its existence, the Gerrard Street Club was never in trouble with the law.

But even with the supper licence our cashier was in no danger of succumbing to wrist fatigue. So we finally had to square up to the realisation that we needed to come up with an offer that the jazz public couldn't refuse. I remembered the Club Eleven and our quixotic letter to Billie Holiday. And I was not unmindful of the fact that in the spring of 1956, the Musicians' Union had lifted its unconditional ban on public performances in Britain by foreign jazz musicians, provided that an exchange deal was arranged. There had, of course, been the exchange between my band and Eddie Condon's in February 1957. The previous year Stan Kenton and Louis Armstrong had visited the UK; Count Basie and Gerry Mulligan played British concerts in April 1957 and Jack Teagarden and Earl Hines appeared in Britain in the winter of the same year.

But thus far no one looked into the possibility of booking American jazz stars for club engagements—and it was Pete King who did an immense amount of pioneering work in that particular field. He negotiated with Harry Francis of the MU and then he went to the United States to talk with representatives of the American Federation of Musicians. It was a long and tedious process, but thanks to Pete's tenacity and determination, and thanks, too, to the brilliant musicianship of Tubby Hayes—who was booked to play the New York Half Note Club in September 1961, thus establishing the required exchange arrangement—we were ultimately able to announce that the great

Zoot Sims would be making a four-week appearance at 39 Gerrard Street in November. That was the beginning of a whole new era for the Club.

Interlude 6

Getting Zoot Sims to appear at the Club was a major coup and a great credit to Pete King's perseverance. And it was thanks to Pete's virtually giving up playing to concentrate on managing the Club that I was able to continue to run a band and do one-night stands around the country. Jazz was still very much a Cinderella music and we got to play in some pretty marginal places. I remember one town where all the girls were terribly unattractive. They held a beauty contest during the dance and nobody won. There was one girl who was so plain that she got obscene phone calls from a guy who reversed the charges—and she accepted them. It seems that when she was a kid her mother had to tie a pork chop round her neck before the dog would play with her.

But our bass player picked up a very nice girl. She was a redhead. No hair. Just a red head. I was told that she played Lady Godiva in a carnival once and everyone looked at the horse.

I wasn't sorry when that gig was over and I was able to get back to London to see Zoot open at the Club. That was really an occasion to remember. . . .

Sixth Set:

Zoot alors!

If I had to name one musician whose playing perfectly exemplified the soaring spirit of freewheeling, free-swinging, therapeutic jazz it would be John Haley 'Zoot' Sims from Inglewood, California. Ever since I had heard him on record as one of the famous 'Four Brothers' saxophone section of the Woody Herman Band of 1947–1949, I had been a fan of his and it was a thrill to see him actually take the stand in my own Club.

It is no secret that European players in those days had an inferiority complex with regard to American musicians and this, when combined with what in some cases was genuine inferiority, often created disastrous tension and atmosphere in pick-up Euro-American groups. Generally speaking, the Americans were entitled to act in a superior way, because many of them *were* musically superior to their European colleagues; but there were certain American jazzmen who clearly took a delight in humiliating European rhythm section players and who seemed more concerned to swagger and to emphasise the discrepancy between their playing and that of their accompanists than to achieve a musical compromise so that the audience at least got some acceptable music.

Zoot Sims was beautifully easy-going and adaptable; he clearly demonstrated right from the start that his primary concern was to find common ground with his rhythm section. It was a good rhythm section by any standards: Stan Tracey on piano, Kenny Napper on bass and the late Jackie Dougan on drums—and it could certainly hold its own with any of the top American horn players. But Stan was always a highly individualistic player—a most accomplished and experienced musician but not everyone's cup of tea as a pianist. Not all of our visitors reacted ecstatically to his playing. But Zoot fitted in superbly and it was altogether a marvellous four weeks. During the run of the gig Zoot made an album for Fontana with Stan's Trio and with Jimmy Deuchar and myself. I think I'm right in saying that this was the first post-war British jazz record to feature an American playing with a British group, except for one I made for Melodisc with American pianist Arnold Ross during a tour of Sweden with Lena Horne.

The booking of Zoot Sims was a success both artistically and commercially. I think we paid Zoot about 300 dollars a week plus his return air fare and we charged members 6s 6d admission and non-members 8s. Our 'office' at the time was little more than a cupboard with such a low ceiling that everybody had to walk around like Quasimodo. The office also had to serve as bandroom and Zoot—over six foot tall—didn't fit into it all that neatly, but he never complained. He didn't even object when some cretinous passer-by on Guy Fawkes Day hurled a smoke bomb into the Club. The place was filled with acrid blue smoke and we had to evacuate the premises for an hour. I think Zoot thought it was some old English custom.

Having built an important bridge with Zoot, Pete and I were determined to maintain as steady a flow of US stars as we could. Except for an occasional session in the Club with the resurrected nine-piece, Pete gave up playing to concentrate full-time on managing the Club—and Zoot's much-acclaimed season paved the way to appearances in the next two or three years by a series of fine musicians who, through no coincidence at all, all happened to be tenor saxophonists— Lucky Thompson, Dexter Gordon, Johnny Griffin, Roland Kirk, Al Cohn, Stan Getz, Bobby Jaspar, Sonny Rollins, Sonny Stitt, Don Byas, Ben Webster and Benny Golson.

Our ambitions extended in other directions, too. We opened branches of the Club in Coventry, Birmingham, Leicester and Nottingham with the idea of booking visiting Americans on a circuit of these venues; but this initiative was relatively short-lived. We really didn't have the time to administer the clubs properly.

It fell to Stan Tracey, as leader of the resident trio, to come to musical terms with the succession of visiting celebrities and also to come to some measure of accommodation with their varied and variable temperaments. Stan has vivid—and, on the whole, extremely affectionate—memories of his days at the Old Place, as 39 Gerrard Street eventually came to be known.

He found the sessions very demanding, but also fulfilling. We were talking about the old days recently and Stan said: 'I know British musicians were supposed to have an inferiority complex, but if I'd felt intimidated, I'd never have stuck it. It was a heavy commitment—almost as heavy as the action of the Club's grand piano. That piano wasn't so much overstrung as overwrought. It took a very special technique and a lot of application to get the best out of it. And, of course, over the years it got worse and worse. In the end, despite deep surgery, it just gave up the ghost.'

Stan remembers lots of good sessions at the Old Place—with people like Zoot, Benny Golson, Art Farmer,

Roland Kirk, Sonny Rollins, Al Cohn, J. J. Johnson, Charlie Mariano, Wes Montgomery and Ben Webster. He says he never got disillusioned about the visitors' music—and only rarely about their personalities. Some British musicians in those days adopted attitudes of inferiority when they played with Americans—but they induced it in themselves. Stan says he never felt inferior—even when the visitors were giving him a hard time.

He told me: 'I didn't let myself be intimidated by the challenge of playing with so-called legends. My adrenalin flowed freely but I never thought of them as legends—just guys who knew what they were about musically and who could play their instruments well. I reasoned that if we were up there with them, we must have been able to take care of business as well. If I hadn't thought that, I would have gone under—but, as it happened, I had to be dragged away every night. It never occurred to me to quit. After all, when I took the job I'd already been playing for fourteen years, so I wasn't exactly a novice.'

Stan says that there were perhaps one or two vocalists he wasn't very comfortable with, but on the whole he found the level of musical compatibility extremely high. Certainly we never had a visiting musician complain that Stan was impossible to work with—even though he claims he sometimes tried to be! He allowed himself to be provoked only on rare occasions. It happened, for example, with the late Don Byas—a man who was endowed with an epic kind of arrogance—and with Lucky Thompson, although the popular story that Lucky once confronted Stan on stage and muttered, 'If you must play crap, play it quietly,' is totally untrue.

Stan found the only way not to let himself be put off by

the 'big time' antics of the guest musicians was to fight them musically. He'd get to know their favourite phrases and would feed them back to them, playing a wrong note at the end as a kind of musical raspberry. They'd be sending him messages in the music and he'd send them right back. Apart from making him feel better, Stan says it was a good musical exercise.

But conflict was really very rare. With a few exceptions, the more talented the star, the easier he was to get on with. Rehearsals took care of tunes with which Stan and his men were not too familiar. They usually had a ball. And the audience at the Old Place was generally very appreciative.

Stan's trio found working full-time at the Club was physically wearing. They used to do normal evening sessions from Monday to Thursday, then an evening performance and an all-nighter on Fridays and Saturdays. Then we had them Sunday afternoons as well. On top of that, when a new guest star arrived for a four-week season, they had to do Monday afternoon rehearsals. For example, they might do a whole month with Freddie Hubbard—a strong, attacking player who loves to set fast tempos. By the end of the engagement they'd be dead tired, shagged out, wiped. . . . Then, before they'd had time to draw a breath, it would be Monday afternoon rehearsal and there would be the incredible Roland Kirk, raring to go and bursting with cosmic energy. No wonder musicians sometimes kicked the cat.

Stan was a tremendous asset to the Club and his philosophical approach to the whole American versus European issue must have sustained him through many daunting situations. What a lot of people failed to realise was that American jazz stars frequently work with local rhythm sections when they tour in the States—and some of those local rhythm sections are sadder than the lowliest of their European counterparts.

But it is certainly true that some British musicians had totally unwarranted feelings of inferiority, especially drummers. There were one or two drummers, according to Stan, who went to pieces on that gig. Most of the time, though, Stan had great musicians with him—Kenny Napper, Malcolm Cecil, Rick Laird and Lennie Bush on bass and Jackie Dougan, Benny Goodman, Ronnie Stephenson and Tony Oxley on drums.

A situation not calculated to restore confidence to the fraternity of drummers (who were still trying to live down the much-quoted line about a certain band consisting of five musicians and a drummer) was one which arose during Dexter Gordon's first stint at the Club in 1962. It happened that, during his stay, Dexter got through eleven drummers—and, inevitably, the word went out that he just couldn't find a British drummer good enough to play with him. Now while it was certainly true that top class British drummers were thinner on the ground—and, in one notable case, in the hair—than other instrumentalists, there were nevertheless a good dozen capable of playing well enough to stop Dexter succumbing to a fit of uncontrollable sobbing. But it just happened that none of them was free to do more than two or three dates—so Benny Goodman had to put in a succession of 'deps'. But, of course, that's not nearly such a good story as 'Dexter Fires Eleven Drummers!'

Certainly, as Stan says, Lucky Thompson and Don Byas could be difficult, but they were such great players that you learned to live with their outsize egos and prickly temperaments.

Lucky Thompson had worked in his time with Lionel

Hampton, Sid Catlett, Don Redman, Lucky Millinder, the famous Billy Eckstine Band of 1944, Dizzy Gillespie and Boyd Raeburn and, as well as being a great tenor player, was a superlative exponent of the soprano saxophone. He'd been living in France since 1957 so his engagement at the Club in June 1962 didn't put too much of a strain on our transport budget. Thompson played magnificently, but I remember I always had to give him twenty minutes' notice before he went on the stand because he was meticulous about cleaning his saxophones. He would clean them with extravagant care before going on and then repeat the whole laborious process after the set.

Thompson was followed into the Club in September 1962 by Dexter Gordon, a bebop-orientated Lester Young disciple from Los Angeles who is a giant, musically and physically. This was the beginning of a long exile in Europe for Dexter which kept him from achieving his full measure of recognition in the United States for fifteen years.

The year 1962 also saw a visit by the quartet of Belgian tenor player Bobby Jaspar—with Rene Thomas on guitar, Benoit Quersin on bass and Daniel Humair on drums—in a reciprocal exchange deal with the Tubby Hayes Quartet. And the year was ushered out in fine style by the return of Zoot Sims with his beautifully compatible tenor-playing partner, Al Cohn.

It was a good year for tenor players—and not a bad year for the Club's one and only attempt to operate as a travel agency. In May we organised an inclusive jazz lovers' package tour on a DC7 to New York offering hotel accommodation and discounts at various jazz clubs for an all-in price of 110 guineas. It was a considerable success but we never repeated it. I don't think Pete was all that fond of adding up guineas.

The first star booking of 1963 was a tenor saxophone player. Johnny Griffin, the little giant from the south side of Chicago, was another American exile in Europe. He'd come over from the States in December 1962 to work at the Blue Note in Paris and we booked him in just before he made a brief return to America. A player with dazzling technique and a profound harmonic grasp, Griffin cut his musical teeth with the Lionel Hampton band and also worked with Thelonious Monk and Art Blakey. He settled permanently in Europe in May 1963 and we brought him over from Paris for a return visit to the Club in December.

I suppose the outstanding event of the year, though, was the appearance of the genuinely inimitable Roland Kirk—a kind of walking three-act opera of a musician who carved himself a unique niche in jazz history by playing three reed instruments simultaneously. Blind since early childhood, Kirk had a passionate commitment to music, a turbulent temperament and boundless energy. His multi-instrumental dexterity was not a gallery-fetching gimmick but just a way of affording himself more channels through which to express his astonishingly abundant musical creativity. As well as the orthodox tenor saxophone and flute, Kirk played such bizarre half-brothers of the reed family as the manzello, stritch and slidesophone. He also played the clarinet, the trumpet and the nose flute. He had developed the art of circular breathing—Harry Carney, Clark Terry and George Coleman are other musicians who mastered the technique—which means that he could inhale air through the nose while expelling it through the mouth, thus being able to sustain a note indefinitely. It was a remarkable experience to watch him at work.

When Roland first came to the Club he did not disguise his reservations about our capacity for fair dealing. He must have encountered some distinctly unscrupulous club owners and bookers in his time because he demanded his money in cash after each performance. We didn't argue—and after three nights he realised that Pete and I were on the level and he trusted us totally from then on. In fact, after that he never came to Europe without telephoning us first and asking for our views on the engagements he'd been offered.

Roland was the first of the new generation of militant black musicians to visit the Club and he was quite obviously on the defensive and expecting the worst when he arrived. He was reassured relatively quickly, and what accelerated his change of mind was undoubtedly the fact that Pete and I were musicians first and businessmen second. That order of priorities has played a great part in enabling us to maintain excellent relationships with musicians over the years.

During his month at the Club, Kirk attracted a great deal of attention. I remember the Beatles came down to see him and were instantly impressed, and there was extensive coverage in the music press because nothing quite like Roland had ever been seen before. As Benny Green has observed, 'he did at times put aside his manzello, his stritch, the swanee whistles, the hunting horns and the assorted special effects, and play an orthodox tenor solo, and it was at these moments that his status became much easier to judge. Kirk at such times is revealed as a highly intelligent, post-Charlie Parker modernist with a fine technique and a lively imagination; a clown who not only dreams of playing Hamlet, but can, when the mood takes him, actually play him'

Steve Race, a pianist and music writer in those days, reviewing Kirk in the *Melody Maker*, saw more of the clown than the virtuoso and likened him to a jazz version of Charlie Cairoli. This was made known to Roland and he was not enchanted. Later on, when he learned that Steve Race was in the audience one night, he invited Steve to sit in on piano. Steve was eventually persuaded to take the stand and Stan Tracey only had a minimal amount of time to explain the treacherous geography, fugitive notes and lamentably uneven touch of the piano. Steve was a more than competent pianist, but he was no match for the combined forces of Roland and that wayward grand piano. Roland gave a convincing demonstration of how to lose a Race while winning, and thus triumphantly set the seal on one of the most musically exciting and challenging four-week engagements in the history of the Club.

Interlude 7

Roland Kirk was three of the most unforgettable musicians we ever had at the Club. The first time he came he introduced the nose flute. The second time he came he demonstrated the ear flute. Quite frankly, I couldn't bear to think what his next flute might be.

But nobody slept while Roland was on. At other times we have had the odd person from Rent-a-Corpse and there are some audiences which amaze me by the way in which they control themselves.

We had a terrible audience the other night. It was the first time I'd seen dead people smoke. There was only one guy applauding and I had to tell him not to clap on his own otherwise the waiter would throw him a fish.

And when I began to do my little chat between sets he started to heckle me. 'Those jokes are terrible,' he shouted. I told him: 'If I want your opinion, sir, I'll give it to you. If you really want me to be funny, I'll have to borrow that suit you're wearing. Somewhere in East London is a Ford Prefect with no seat covers.'

I think his problem was that he was a little stoned on a special drink we'd been serving that night—it was a mixture of one part muscatel and one part hock. We call it 'muck'.

Generally speaking we get very few drunks at the Club—sometimes it seems that most of the audience has been drinking cement—and we get very few unpleasant incidents considering we're in the heart of Soho. The only serious case I can remember was one which I'll tell you about in the next set.

Seventh Set:

So far, Soho good

Between Johnny Griffin's first appearance at the Club in February 1963 and the astonishing début of Roland Kirk, we had a succession of singers of highly diverse styles. I must confess that this was due less to my abiding interest in the vocal arts than to the fact that there were not the same restrictions on performances by foreign vocalists in Britain as there were on foreign instrumentalists.

Babs Gonzales, one of the pioneers among the bebop scat vocalists, appeared first; then came Betty Bennett, who was once married to André Previn; and then another fine American jazz singer who made a big impression on the London jazz scene, Joy Marshall.

Since the breakup of the Jazz Couriers I had been running a small group featuring Ronnie Ross and Jimmy Deuchar and in June 1963 we followed in the footsteps of Tubby Hayes and made an appearance at the New York Half Note Club. It was a most rewarding experience and I felt much more comfortable in those surroundings than I had on that 1957 tour with the rock 'n' roll package.

Throughout the year we devoted every spare penny towards improving the amenities of the Club. We started offering a more elaborate menu by simply sending out to the various nearby restaurants. I remember we grandly announced in our *Melody Maker* ads: 'Choice of English and Indian Cuisines'—and it was good Indian food, too, obtained from the Curry Centre just across the road—none of your stoat vindaloo and mattress curry (made with Dunlopilau rice).

We also redecorated the place and it was while we were working on this first repaint job that a guy called Gypsy Larry wandered in off the street and asked if we wanted any help. We stuck a paintbrush in his hand, gave him a pot of paint and told him to paint anything that wasn't moving. He stayed all day—and for the next twelve years. I think he'd originally worked as a road manager for a couple of skiffle groups. He became something of an institution at the Club although we never really quite worked out exactly what his function was. When visitors asked him, he would say, confidently, that he 'worked the lights'. Then there was Alex, our cloakroom attendant. Alex had the sort of face that only a near-sighted mother could love, but he was convinced that he was cut out to be a male model. While he was waiting to be discovered he worked in the daytime as a gravedigger.

If you run a club in the heart of Soho you are bound to attract characters who are, to say the least, out of the ordinary; there is also the constant possibility of having to contend with drunks and general trouble-makers. But in twenty years we have had surprisingly little aggravation. There has never been a really serious fight in the Club—God knows why we spent all that money on balsa wood furniture—and we have rarely been troubled by undesirable characters. I think that because Pete and I have worked in the West End all our lives, we are well-known to some of the top hoods and villains and they leave us alone. Working around Soho as a musician, you inevitably come into contact with the underworld. I used to gamble with some of the villains in the old days and I'm still quite friendly with a couple of big-time gangsters. The villains will do all kinds of evil things to each other, but it always seemed to be part of their code never to give musicians a hard time. The Soho scene was never remotely like Chicago in the days of Al Capone when the hoods used to tell the bandleaders to keep playing their tune . . . or else. In fact sometimes when my band is working at the Club before a certain kind of audience, we get the impression that we're likely to be in trouble if we *start* playing.

The one really ugly incident I remember—I'll never forget it because it scared the pot out of me—occurred at the Old Place one evening. A really tough-looking villain—'with well-cut suit and face to match,' to use Flash Winstone's elegant phrase—came down the stairs, strode through the door, went up to the coffee bar and growled in a voice that was one part Bow and three parts Bell's, 'Give us a f...in' cup of coffee.'

I said to him, 'Sorry, sir. If you want to come into the Club you must buy a ticket.'

He took absolutely no notice of me but simply repeated to the guy on the coffee bar, 'Give us a f...in' cup of coffee,' shouting this time.

'If you won't buy a ticket,' I said, 'I'm afraid I'll have to ask you to leave.' Actually by now I was afraid, period, because I could smell trouble.

'F... the ticket,' he snarled. 'I want a f...in' cup of coffee.'

'If you don't leave I'll have to call the law,' I told him, knowing as I said it that far from deterring the drunk the threat would probably provoke him into further nastiness. So I headed for the door in search of a copper. I'd just about reached the door when I heard Chick, our cashier, shout, 'Look out, Ronnie, he's got a gun!'

74

I whirled around and saw Chick struggling with the guy, holding his gun arm from behind with his right hand and hooking his left arm around the drunk's throat. I sprang forward and dived for the gun and somehow we wrestled the guy to the floor and got the gun away. Someone called the police and we managed to keep the geezer under control until they arrived.

He was arrested and charged and I eventually had to go to Bow Street Magistrates' Court to give evidence. It turned out that the guy had yards of 'form'—armed robbery, grievous bodily harm and various other peccadilloes—and he went down for seven years. Outside the court some of his relatives—two brothers and a sister—came up to me and one of the brothers muttered grimly, 'What did you 'ave to call the f...in' law for? Why didn't you f...in' just sling 'im f...in' out?' This picturesque mode of speech seemed to run in the family.

'Look,' I said, uneasily. 'I'm very sorry but we're not tearaways and he *was* waving a gun about. . . .'

'Aw f... off!' said the brother, disgustedly.

I must say that for quite a while after that free and frank exchange of views I used to get a prickly sensation in the nape of the neck whenever I heard quickening footsteps behind me. But, happily, I didn't fall victim to any vengeance plot. As a matter of fact, the hood came back to see me years later. I was a bit disconcerted when he marched into the Club—but he was quite inoffensive.

'Hallo. Er . . . just come out. I'm f...in' skint, ain't I? What about it?'

I gave him a fiver and he disappeared. He collected two more fivers on subsequent visits but on the fourth appearance I told him: 'Listen, don't come back again.' And he never did.

75

That was the only really scary thing that has happened in twenty years, I'm delighted to say. Despite the fact that we've always been in darkest Soho, in the thick of the strip clubs, the near-beer joints, the porn cinemas and the numerous branches of that well-known retail newsagent partnership, Sid Books & Alf Mags, we have had less bovver than you get in the average old folks home.

In fact, when Pete and I were looking for bigger premises in 1965, a couple of heavies came up to us one night and said they would pass the word on to an organisation that might be able to help us. A few nights later we had a call to say that somebody would be coming to the Club to take us to see some premises in Knightsbridge. An hour later one of the Kray twins came in and drove us round to see a club they ran called Esmeralda's Barn. As it turned out it really wasn't what we were looking for—but, we certainly weren't anticipating help from that quarter when we started our search for a larger room.

When we eventually moved to Frith Street, Pete and I were presented with a jereboam of champagne on opening night by Albert Dimes. We resolved to open it when we got out of debt. It's still in the cellar.

Although the Club has had a remarkably trouble-free record there have been occasions when we've had disturbances from musicians. 6 March, 1964 saw the arrival at the Club for a four-week season of one of the most brilliant tenor saxophonists of all time—Stan Getz. Another former member of Woody Herman's 'Four Brothers' saxophone team, which he joined as a twenty-year-old, Getz has been internationally recognised as one of the great jazz virtuosi for the past twenty-five years. He is a master technician, a brilliant, melodic improviser and an artist of impeccable taste. His arrival at the Club coincided

76

with the immense new impetus which had been given to his career by his involvement in the blending of Brazilian music with jazz to produce what became known as the bossa nova. His 1962 'Jazz Samba' album with Charlie Byrd was to become one of the biggest-selling jazz albums of all time.

Stan was spellbinding as a musician, but it was not unknown for him to be a shade temperamental and his début at the Club was not without its problems.

Because of certain difficulties with Customs and Immigration on a previous visit to Britain for a Jazz At The Philharmonic tour, Stan had been barred from return visits. But early in 1964 Pete and I decided we would have a stab at getting him a working permit. Ever since we first got the OK to bring Americans in, we had been talking about booking Stan, but we knew we couldn't stretch our meagre funds to cover the kind of fee he would require. And with the recent boost to his career provided by the bossa nova boom, he looked to be even further out of our reach. But we tried for a permit just for the hell of it—and to our immense surprise, it was granted. Pete called Stan in New York and, using his loaf in the best East End fashion, said, 'If by any chance, Stan, we *were* able to get a work permit for you, how much would you want to work at the Club for a month? And before you answer, let me tell you that the most we could afford would be 300 dollars a week.'

Stan was all sweet reasonableness. 'If you can get a permit, Pete,' he said, 'I'll accept that fee.' That's how certain he was that he wouldn't be allowed to work in Britain. But, to give him credit, when we did produce the work permit, he kept his word—although I think he suspected that Pete had pulled a fast one.

He came into the Club to rehearse three days before he was due to open. We were doing some hurried decoration and repairs in order to have the place looking reasonable for Stan's opening. We were having to work pretty fast because we still had to open the Club that night. Pete was doing a repair job on a table and, inevitably, making a bit of noise—and Stan got very angry claiming that it was impossible to rehearse under such conditions. Pete apologised and explained that the work just had to be done—but Stan was really upset and spent the next few days convinced that Pete had been trying to sabotage his rehearsal.

The Club was packed every night during Stan's engagement, and every night we had to go through the same ritual to get him on stage. I'd be on the stand announcing him and Pete would bring him from the back office, clearing a path through the crowd.

As time went on, Stan seemed to get more and more leisurely in making his way from the back office to the bandstand and I'd be standing like an idiot on stage confronting an increasingly restive audience. Of course, that sort of behaviour is the prerogative of a great artist and it's a well-known show business device to keep the audience on their toes and build up excitement; but Pete King doesn't have a lot of time for such inessential stratagems and after a couple of weeks he got pretty fed up with Stan's lingering, languorous mode of taking the stage. He came to me one evening and said, 'Ronnie, I've just got to keep out of Stan's way otherwise I'm likely to lose my temper.'

Well, in the end he did lose his temper and a majestic shout-up ensued. Pete unloaded all the antagonism that had been building up inside him for weeks and Stan, not unnaturally, retaliated with equal vigour. I came on the

78

scene just at the point when Stan's denigration of Pete was reaching a crescendo and, seeing my friend and partner under such a savage verbal attack I started to have a thorough go at Stan. It all got very heated, but I guess it did us all good to get the frustration out of our systems because when the dust had settled we stood around looking at each other sheepishly and realised that we somehow didn't have problems any more. That concerto for three raised voices really cleared the air and from that point on we had a very good relationship.

The very next day I was supposed to do a television show with Tubby Hayes and a couple of other bands, but as I was getting into my car, I felt this acute stabbing pain in my back. I had slipped a disc—and I was obliged to spend the next ten days or so on my back. I'm still convinced that I sustained the slipped disc because of bending over backwards to please Stan Getz.

There were one or two difficult moments on the bandstand, too. Musicians like Stan set very high standards for themselves and expect similar levels of musicianship from their accompanists. Stan Tracey thinks that Stan Getz was probably the toughest and most demanding American jazzman he ever had to work with. But by the time Getz came to the Club, Stan's trio was pretty well equipped to cope with the most awkward of visiting stars, both on a musical and personality level. If they suspected that an American was coming in with the intention of cutting loose on the stand and expecting the British lads to cower and cringe in trepidation, then Stan and his men were hostile to him almost before his plane touched down at Heathrow.

There would be an inner hostility but an outward impassivity from the trio as they waited for the vistor to make the first move. If it was a friendly, amiable move, the trio warmed to him. If it was an unfriendly, upstaging kind of move, then it was likely to trigger off a war of attrition.

Stan recalls the time when Stan Getz once offered a thoroughly scurrilous comment on the stand about his piano playing. Says Stan:

'I replied with a carefully considered pearl of English repartee. "Bollocks," I said.'

I wish I'd thought of that.

Interlude 8

As the years went by the quality of the food we served at the Club improved tremendously. And today we never get complaints about the food. We get a few people throwing up—but no complaints.

You've probably gathered by now from these little interludes between sets that I'm not a professional comedian; but we do have a fantastic professional comedian at the Club. We call him the chef.

He's rather an unusual guy—he's half black and half Japanese and every 7 December he attacks Pearl Bailey.

He got married three weeks ago, and already he can hear the patter of tiny feet around the house. His mother-in-law's a dwarf. And she's very ugly. It seems her husband took her on a very expensive holiday round the world rather than kiss her goodbye.

Which reminds me of that dramatic day in March 1965 when we kissed goodbye to our veteran piano. Nobody reported seeing Stan Tracey wipe away a fugitive tear. . .

Eighth Set:

Bill and Ben

Another superlative saxophone technician—Sonny Stitt—followed Stan Getz into the Club in May and proceeded to dazzle us all with his mastery of chord changes and his Charlie Parker-inspired bebop lines. He was succeeded by one of my favourite jazz singers, Jimmy Witherspoon, who appeared at the Club with my band as a backing group. I'll never forget that engagement because Jimmy had a habit of making conversational asides to me on stage between lines of the blues. He'd start out singing, *'Got the blues in the mornin'. . .'* then turn to me and rattle off at a furious pace, 'Hey Ronnie, Basie wants me to go to Japan . . .

'Got the blues in the evenin' . . .

But I ain't goin' 'cause he don't pay enough money . . .

'Got the blues all night long. . .'

After Spoon, came one of the great jazz trumpeters of the day, Donald Byrd, and then one of the pioneers of modern jazz trombone, J. J. Johnson. And the year was seen out in magnificent style by the first appearance of the incomparable Ben Webster, a man of imposing physical and artistic stature who in the words of jazz writer Leonard Feather, belonged 'along with Coleman Hawkins and Chu Berry, among the earliest figures to bring full maturity to the tenor saxophone.' Ben had been a prominent member of the Duke Ellington Orchestra on and off for thirteen years and was universally regarded as having one of the richest, most ravishing saxophone sounds in jazz, particularly on ballads. He was a gentle, lovable man for the most part whose one character flaw was a tendency to get comprehensively bombed on gin for days at a time.

Ben hated flying, so he came to Britain from New York by boat and Pete and I drove down to Southampton in a Mini to meet him. We'd had a somewhat garbled telephone call from him in Cherbourg—which apprised us of nothing except that he'd clearly spent a considerable amount of time in the bar—but when he came off the boat at Southampton he seemed quite straight and steady, if a little subdued. We helped squeeze his sixteen stones into the back seat of the Mini and set off back for London. Within minutes Ben had dozed off and was snoring vigorously. Then suddenly, after we'd been travelling for half an hour, he woke up and roared: 'Well, give them what they want—as long as they don't want too much!' Then he lapsed immediately back into a sound sleep. Pete and I exchanged glances, shrugged, and wondered what we were getting ourselves into.

But Ben played superbly during that first engagement, even though at fifty-four he was beginning to lose some of his agility on the instrument. He settled permanently in Europe after his début at the Club and he played for us on a number of subsequent occasions before his death in Amsterdam in September 1973. Towards the end of his life his legs got very bad and he used to have to play sitting on a chair. Nine times out of ten when he arrived for work he would be straight, but on the odd occasion he would come in utterly plastered. He'd be standing by me at the side of the stage as I announced him and I'd hear him mutter, 'Now, if I can just make it to that chair . . .'

He played a two-week date for us at the Frith Street Club a few years back and he was wonderful—completely sober all the time. But when he finished the engagement he stayed on in London for a while. One night he came into the Club as tired as a newt and ran into the singer Billy Eckstine, an old friend Ben hadn't seen in years. They fell on each other's necks, hugged each other and rolled around the Club in blissful euphoria. Then they went to the bar and stood there talking and drinking until we closed.

Two days later Ben came into the Club completely sober. I said, 'Hey, Ben, it must have been great seeing Billy the other night after all those years.'

'Billy?' Ben answered. 'Billy who?'

'Billy Eckstine.'

'Billy *Eckstine*!' Ben roared incredulously. 'Are you kidding? I ain't seen Billy in seven years.'

There were other times when Ben gave the impression that he was more juiced than he actually was—perhaps because he rather liked to be saved the trouble of having to fend for himself. I remember one night round about closing time when Ben was legless. Pete and I were holding him up and helping him towards the door. He was a dead weight and apparently very close to unconsciousness with his head lolling forward. We stopped momentarily to let one of our pretty waitresses by and Ben suddenly lifted his head and exclaimed, wide-eyed, 'Just *look* at the tits on that child!' Then his head slumped forward, and he was apparently out to lunch once again.

Jimmy Parsons, who helped run our booking agency between 1966 and 1971 and arranged tours for some of the jazz artists appearing at the Club, has many fond memories of Ben Webster on tour. They were in Coventry on one occasion and Ben, an enthusiastic photographer, went with Jimmy the morning after the gig to Coventry Cathedral, intent on taking pictures of the interior. As soon as they arrived Jimmy spotted a very emphatic sign forbidding the use of cameras in the cathedral without written permission. Ben was unimpressed. He went in, checking his lenses, winding on film and consulting his light meter—and immediately caught the beady eye of a tiny friar who could not have been more than four feet seven inches tall. The friar waved an admonishing finger and whispered, 'No photos.' Ben and Jimmy moved slowly up the aisle amid a crowd of visitors, Ben continually fiddling with his cameras and the friar hard behind, now jumping up and down to catch the first sign of an attempt by Ben to take a photograph. Ben saw this movement out of the corner of his eye, turned round and glared at the friar, and then announced to Jimmy, with a roar that reverberated throughout that hallowed house of God: 'Hey, Jim, that evil mother-f. . .er is looking at me!'

After Ben settled on the continent, he would come to London by the boat train whenever he had a British tour. There was one Sunday when Jimmy Parsons went to meet the train at Victoria but failed to spot Ben among the passengers—and Ben, with his massive corpulence and his inevitable trilby hat was not easy to overlook. Jimmy asked the ticket collector if he might move on to the platform to see if Ben was still on the train. He walked up the platform checking the carriages. In the compartment immediately adjoining the buffet car he saw Ben slumped, half dressed, on the seat. His suitcase was open and half the contents were strewn over the floor. Ben was bombed. Jimmy climbed aboard, got a cheery greeting from Ben and a pressing invitation to have a slug of gin. 'Later, Ben.' Jimmy said—and then set about trying to dislodge him from the compartment. But Ben was in no hurry to move—even though the train was about to go into a siding. Jimmy, a slightly-built guy, had no option but to summon help. He found the guard but the man was clearly uneasy at the thought of trying to manipulate such a large quantity of drunken saxophonist through the carriage door. Ben received him warmly: 'Hello, my man—hey, have a little taste,' he said proffering the gin bottle. The guard backed away fearfully, then fled down the platform. Minutes later two policemen arrived; one of them, in his fifties, was understanding and sympathetic—the other, much younger, was officious and rather churlish. Ben remained his imperturbably affable self. 'Well, Jim, now here's the po-lice come to join my little party. Hey, my man, have a taste. . . .'

Somehow the three of them got Ben on to the platform and transported him by parcel trolley to Jimmy's car. 'Hey, my man,' Ben said to the older policeman, 'do you have kids?' The copper said he did, a boy and a girl, and Ben beamed at him and said, 'Well, my man, you can tell your kids that you've brought them a present from Ben Webster—you're a nice po-liceman.' And Ben pressed a £10 note into the fist of the copper.

Whenever we had to make a change in the programme for one reason or another, it became part of my routine to announce that the guy who was billed to appear was unable to make it because he'd been taken suddenly drunk. That literally happened with Ben on one occasion. People started coming into the Club that evening to hear the Ben Webster Quartet but found when they got to their seats that all the Club was offering was Ben's rhythm section. They were unaware that the prostrate, bulky and insensible form they had been stepping over in the foyer was the bandleader, in an advanced state of bibulous oblivion.

But for all his bouts of prodigious drinking, Ben was a wonderful person and a giant of jazz for whom Pete and I always had a deep affection.

Early in 1965 another giant made his début at the Club—a saxophonist, of course. Theodore Walter 'Sonny' Rollins, for a long time a major idol of mine. A man of unorthodox inclinations, Rollins is an important innovator who brings an intense conviction to everything he does. He would sometimes play continuously throughout one set, switching from one tune to another without a break, and he had a predilection for taking the most unlikely tunes—like 'There's No Business Like Show Business', 'Count Your Blessings' and 'Sonny Boy'—and converting them into jazz vehicles.

When Sonny arrived at the Club to rehearse with Stan Tracey's trio, he strolled about the place playing the odd note and adjusting his reed while Stan and his men sat around doing nothing. Then eventually Rollins said, 'OK, let's try a ballad—"Prelude To A Kiss".' They rehearsed that tune for an hour, just playing chorus after chorus—and then Sonny decided the rehearsal was over. And with exquisite logic he went through the whole four-week engagement without ever calling the one tune the band had rehearsed. An unconventional chap, Sonny. Few people who witnessed it will forget the night be began his set by starting to play inside a London taxi cab, blowing his way across the pavement, into the Club and on to the stage. He was unconventional, too, in matters of hairstyling at that time—he had shaved his head and was strongly into mysticism. It seemed to entail a life of self-denial because after the gig he would head straight back to his hotel and decline to dissipate like a normal musician. It seemed to be all meditation and macrobiotic food and towards the end of the engagement I began to feel quite sorry for him. There was an all-night café in Windmill Street which had a billiard hall. It was frequented by taxi drivers and we often used to hang out there after the Club closed. One night I remember saying to Sonny, 'We're going on to this all-night billiard hall after we close—why don't you join us? You can get a good meal there and play billiards—you'll see a slice of English life.'

'I don't think so,' said Sonny gently. Then he added, with just the barest hint of a twinkle in his eye, 'But you go ahead—and have a nice slice.'

March 1965 was another landmark in the Club's history because it saw the first visit to Gerrard Street of a top American pianist and the first by a complete American group—the Bill Evans Trio, with Chuck Israels on bass and Larry Bunker on drums. Bill Evans had won tremendous critical acclaim with his first albums for the Riverside label in the mid-fifties on which he displayed a technical mastery of the keyboard and a delicate, thoughtful, impressionist style which brought a new lyricism to the art of jazz piano. When we booked Bill, Pete and I knew that common decency demanded that a player of his finesse and sensitivity had to be provided with a good piano. There was a firm in Covent Garden that advertised pianos for hire—so Pete and I went and picked one out. Then we had the battle-scarred brute with which Stan Tracey had waged such valiant combat with for so long, taken out and sold. We arranged to have the new piano delivered on the afternoon of the Monday on which the

Bill Evans Trio was booked to open.

At about lunchtime on that Monday a representative of the hire firm came to inspect the Club—and when he saw the narrow steps leading down to the basement and observed the sign that announced that ours was a jazz club, his jaw sagged in disbelief. Surely we did not expect him to allow one of his fine instruments to be installed in such a disreputable sink of iniquity? His expression clearly announced that he had visions of half-naked girls dancing on the piano and of carousing ruffians pouring beer into it.

'Even if we could get it down the stairs. I wouldn't allow one of our pianos in this place', he exclaimed, registering the shocked horror of a man who has just seen a television reading of Eskimo Nell by Mary Whitehouse.

Well, for the next hour, Pete King and I pleaded with the guy, using all the guile, blandishments and downright duplicity we could summon. We had a little bit of money in hand so we offered to give him £100 deposit to cover any possible damage. No dice. OK, then, we said, we'll *buy* the piano. Name your price.

'Cash?' he asked.

'Well—£100 in cash and a post-dated cheque for the balance.'

'No deal. In any case, it will never go down those stairs.'

We went over and over the same ground trying to get the guy to change his mind. We explained we had one of the world's finest pianists arriving to play in a matter of hours and, as yet, we had nothing for him to play on. We appealed to his better nature, we reasoned patiently with him, we offered him our undying gratitude and our perpetual custom, free life membership. Everything. We were totally desperate by now. But he was absolutely unyielding. So Pete, always a calm man in a crisis, summoned up his last reserves of diplomatic ingenuity, put his face very close to the guy's ear and said with solemn and measured deliberation, 'Oi. F. . . off!'

That brought immense relief but it didn't solve our problem. Bill Evans arrived and we explained the situation to him. We said we'd keep trying. A place in the Edgware Road offered us a mini piano, but we explained to the Austrian saleslady that we really couldn't ask the great Bill Evans to play a dwarf instrument. 'Vy not?' she said, 'He vill be able to see his boys over ze top.'

Happily the day was saved by pianist Alan Clare who managed to produce a good grand piano from somewhere or other. And Bill Evans really made it sing.

The astonishing self-taught guitarist Wes Montgomery followed Bill Evans into the Club and stunned everybody with his virtuosity. Then Ben Webster returned, to be followed by Al Cohn and Zoot Sims and then the début of one of the most mellifluous of trumpet and fluegelhorn players, Art Farmer. Don Byas, a former Count Basie, Andy Kirk, Lucky Millinder and Dizzy Gillespie sideman who had long been resident in Europe, made his début at the Club in August 1965 and was followed by Benny Golson, also a tenor saxophonist, who was trying to tread a stylistic path between Lucky Thompson and John Coltrane.

The Club was certainly presenting some illustrious names but as a business venture it was still decidedly shaky. The high cost of booking top American artists allied to our limited seating capacity meant that the profit margin—when there *was* a profit—was extremely meagre. It has been said that Pete and I used to meet every Sunday at 3 am to decide whether we could afford to open the following Monday—and that is not too far from the truth. For some months now we had recognised that if we were to keep going, we would have to find bigger premises so that we could accommodate larger audiences—and in the summer of 1965 we found an ideal location at 47 Frith Street, just a few hundred yards away.

We had to raise something like £35,000 in order to convert and decorate the premises and we were extremely lucky to have a good friend in Harold Davison, a promoter who has always had a soft spot for jazz. We made him an offer he could easily refuse—but he still lent us the money. Without that generous help there would be no Ronnie Scott's Club today.

The Old Place closed on 27 November, 1965—closed as it had opened, six years earlier, with a tenor saxophonist. Benny Golson was the last American jazzman to play at 39 Gerrard Street. The race to get the new premises open before Christmas was an immensely hectic one. We had a team of Irish labourers working for us and with two days to go before our scheduled opening on Friday, 17 December, we knew that the only way we could possibly make it was to have the builders work solidly through the next forty eight hours. So I went down to the East End and got about fifty black bombers—rather powerful 'uppers'—and we fed them to our Irish squad. The result was fantastic—it was like watching a speeded-up film. Pete and I went home early on Friday morning to get a few hours sleep, leaving the place looking like the aftermath of a minor earthquake. We came back the next day and the Irish guys were still in a boisterous frenzy of drilling, hammering, sawing, planning, accompanied by a fervour of babbling conversation prodigiously laced with expletives.

Miraculously we opened that night—and naturally enough, we featured a tenor saxophonist, Yusef Lateef. He was rather a special visitor however, because he also played oboe and flute—an excellent musician. Opposite him was singer Ernestine Anderson, a lady who had sung with Johnny Otis and Lionel Hampton. Our Irish friends had done their level best, but there were one or two little finishing touches which had had to be foregone. Bob Dawbarn of the *Melody Maker*, reporting the opening night of the new premises, wrote: 'After a three-week pause the new Ronnie Scott's Club opened in Frith Street, two hours late, with Yusef Lateef, Ernestine Anderson and a novel ventilation system—no front door.'

There were hardly any electricity circuits working so we had candles on the tables. There were wires trailing everywhere and it was a few days before we were able to offer separate ladies' and men's lavatories. It was all very Bohemian for a while.

Through 1966 we had return visits from Ernestine Anderson, Sonny Rollins, Jimmy Witherspoon, Freddie Hubbard, Roland Kirk, Johnny Griffin and Ben Webster and débuts by Sheila Jordan, Blossom Dearie, Lee Konitz, Jim Hall, Charlie Mariano, the Horace Silver Quintet, Marian Montgomery, and the controversial Ornette Coleman. Coleman was the first real avant garde player to appear at the Club. He had been hailed by John Lewis of the Modern Jazz Quartet as 'doing the only really new thing in jazz since the innovations of Dizzy Gillespie and Charlie Parker in the forties and since Thelonious Monk.' However Monk, himself something of a high priest of modern jazz, was not much impressed when he came to hear Ornette at the Club. For Monk, one of the most notable eccentrics in jazz, the whole world is innocent of ashtrays. So he sat at a table smoking cigarettes one after another and throwing the lighted dog ends unconcernedly over his shoulder. Ornette Coleman's principal instrument was alto saxophone, but he also had a perfunctory stab at playing trumpet and left-handed violin. After a somewhat noisy and self-indulgent set, Monk called to Coleman, 'Hey, if you want a fiddle in the band, why don't you get yourself a fiddle player? And if you want a trumpet in the band, get yourself a trumpet player.' It is very rare in my experience for musicians publicly to disparage their peers—but Monk always made his own rules.

Although we had shut up shop in Gerrard Street, Pete and I planned to reopen the basement as a place in which to present some of the excellent younger musicians who were coming on to the British jazz scene—and we finally took the step in September 1966. Absolutely no prizes for guessing that the first attraction was a tenor saxophonist—West Indian Harold McNair, a most gifted player who doubled on flute. Harold was never to achieve his true potential however because he died of cancer in March 1971 at the age of forty.

For the next two years—until the lease ran out and we were unable to afford to renew it at treble the previous figure—the Old Place presented some outstanding musicians, including Graham Collier, Mike Osborne, John Surman, Chris McGregor, Dudu Pukwana, Evan Parker, Tony Oxley and Mike Westbrook. It ran at a loss, but we were happy to subsidise it as long as we could afford to.

The bewildering complexities of the British licensing laws are such that Pete and I—being non-drinkers—have never begun to comprehend them, but we did manage to determine that part of the price our guests had to pay during the sixties for being able to take alcoholic refreshment until three in the morning was that they had to consume some food as well. We had what was called a supper licence but for the convenience of guests who came into the club bulging with highly-seasoned food from the local Soho restaurants, we quickly reduced 'supper' to a sandwich or a plate of biscuits and cheese. There were those ungracious clients who were heard to observe on occasion that their cheese sandwich had looked a lot better when it had first been served to them three weeks earlier. It was a curious ritual, but Pete and I are law-abiding chaps, so we conformed. However, we were apparently breaking the law in some insidious way because one night in October, 1966, we received the supreme accolade for an after-hours club—a police raid. And I must say the law timed it beautifully, because they descended on us right in the middle of a Roland Kirk set. The result was indescribable chaos.

Roland at this time was heavily into penny whistles—in addition to his twenty-three or so regular instruments—and at the beginning of every set he would hand whistles round to everyone in the audience and invite them to play along. It was when this massed penny whistle choir was in full and shrilly discordant cry that the twenty plain-clothed policemen burst into the Club blowing their own whistles. Roland, on stage, hadn't the remotest idea what was happening but he seemed not unpleased by the augmentation to his penny whistle section and he urged the audience on to greater prodigies of piping virtuosity. The police were extremely irked. One of them said to me, 'Tell that man to stop playing.' I replied: 'You tell him.'

Eventually calm was restored, names and addresses were taken and we were summoned for some breach of the licensing laws and fined £250. After that we applied for, and got, a different kind of licence, so we put the cheese sandwiches back into store.

The début of the Horace Silver Quintet at the Frith Street Club on 17 September, 1966, was another milestone in that it was the first time so large a group had been imported from the States. The band featured Woody Shaw on trumpet and Tyrone Washington on tenor saxophone and played for four weeks. It was when we closed after Silver's opening night that an electric fault on a beer cooler in the service area caused a serious fire which did hundreds of pounds' worth of damage before it was brought under control. I think that's about the only major administrative mistake Pete King has made in twenty years. The fire was supposed to be the following week.

Interlude 9

Taking on bigger premises represented a big gamble, but, like my dad, I've always been a bit of a gambler and I must say I usually have a lot of luck. Bad, mostly. I've been known to stop a runaway horse dead in its tracks just by putting money on it.

With the larger venue we engaged more staff. In 1966 we employed six waitresses and I believe three of them actually worked in the Club. On the whole our staff were pretty loyal and stayed with us—although we did have a lavatory attendant once who quit because he couldn't stand the smell of the kitchen.

We also took on a Hungarian waiter. He didn't understand the social security system when he first started to work for us and he used to stick Green Shield stamps on his insurance card. He got nicked for it—and the judge gave him six months. And a tea set.

We also had a rather strange Italian waiter working for us briefly. He told us his previous job was as a road sweeper. In Venice.

But Luigi never got anything right. In fact, the only time he was right in his whole life was the one occasion when he thought he was wrong.

And I'll tell you, there were a lot of people who thought we were wrong—and insane—when we decided in 1968 to acquire the premises next door and redesign the Club as a three-storey entertainment complex. . . .

I preferred The Old Place— it was more uncomfortable . .

Ninth Set:

Miles gets the brush

As Pete and I waged the constant battle to balance the books, we came up from time to time with ideas for different ventures which we could run in association with the Club. We'd tried a daytime jazz college at the Gerrard Street premises and we'd had quite a good response; but the problem was that all the pupils were at different stages of development and we didn't really have adequate space. Another enterprise we ran fairly successfully for a couple of years was a record shop dealing in special jazz imports. But our main preoccupation was always to present the best in jazz in the best possible surroundings, and with the new premises we were able to be more ambitious.

In the spring of 1967 we achieved another 'first' when we had an entire American big band play the Club for two nights—the band led and driven by the indefatigable Buddy Rich, one of the most illustrious drummers in jazz. Those performances paved the way for a whole succession of big bands over the next decade. The list is impressive—the Clarke-Boland Band, Woody Herman, Peter Herbolzheimer's Rhythm Combination & Brass, Johnny Dankworth, Maynard Ferguson, the Pasadena Roof Orchestra, Harry James, Tommy Dorsey, Thad Jones-Mel Lewis, Count Basie and Stan Kenton.

Another major event of 1967 was the first appearance at the Club by the inventor of the jazz tenor saxophone—Coleman Hawkins. Hawk made his début on 27 November, his appearance following an autumn jazz festival at the Club which had featured Clark Terry and Bob Brookmeyer, Bill Evans, Gary Burton and the controversial Archie Shepp. Coleman Hawkins was fantastic—he was sixty-three years-old when he made his Club début but he was still playing with that enormous, commanding sound and with a blow-torch intensity. He had an absolutely towering ego—but I suppose his unchallenged position in the tenor saxophone hierarchy entitled him to a degree of vaingloriousness. I remember that trumpeter Dennis Rose approached Hawk during his engagement at the Club and said to him: 'When Ben Webster was here a couple of weeks ago, he used to let musicians sit in with him. Why don't you?' Hawk answered with gruff contempt: 'Ben needs 'em; I don't.'

Actually Ben and Bean—as Hawkins was known —were the best of friends and they'd spend hours in the dressing room talking over old times. How I wish I'd had a tape recorder handy on those occasions! They were both colossal drinkers, but whereas Ben used to drink himself into insensibility, Hawk never seemed to succumb. He would get through two bottles of Remy Martin a day, drinking it alternately with draughts from a pitcher of iced water. I never saw him eat anything other than minestrone soup and it is a miracle to me that he survived so long.

One night Hawk and Ben were reminiscing when Stan Getz came into the dressing room to pay his respects. As soon as Stan entered Ben let loose a torrent of obscenities, got to his feet and pinned Getz against the wall. He might well have done Getz a serious injury—but we managed to calm Ben down and restore order. I discovered afterwards that Ben had been under the false impression that Stan had made some disparaging remarks about one of Ben's great friends—another musician—and Ben wasn't going to stand for that.

Hawkins was a frail old man nearing the end of his life at this time, but he had a tremendous inner strength. Jimmy Parsons remembers travelling with him by train to a gig in Newcastle. Hawk bought two bottles of Remy Martin from an off licence before catching the train and finished one of them during the journey. The other one was despatched during the concert, and then on return to the hotel, Hawk decided it was time for 'a little taste' and lowered a further batch of cognacs. Jimmy Parsons, who by this time had had more brandy than he could comfortably handle, retired to bed at 3 am leaving Hawkins still at the bar. He and Hawk had adjoining rooms in the hotel and a couple of hours later Parsons was awakened by a voice next door asking the telephone operator for room service. 'Send me up a pitcher of iced water and a bottle of Remy Martin,' he heard Hawk say—and, at five in the morning in this English provincial hotel, the brandy was duly delivered!

Later on our agency set up a tour for Ben Webster and we had the idea of having his greater mentor, Coleman Hawkins, join him on one of the dates—at a university in the home counties. At this time, though, Hawk was really seriously ill and we decided to cancel the appearance. But Hawkins wouldn't hear of it. 'I'm going to work with my man, Ben,' he said. 'I'm not going to let the people down.' He was so ill when Jimmy Parsons and Jeff Ellison, our doorman, got him to the gig that a doctor was summoned. He diagnosed pneumonia, administered an injection of antibiotics and adrenalin and recommended that Hawk be taken to hospital. But Hawk insisted that he was going to play with Ben Webster. Jimmy and Jeff virtually had to carry Hawk on stage and they were both desperately sad to see this great jazz performer in such a critical state. He was fighting for breath and was clearly about to make a tragic spectacle of himself.

Jimmy and Jeff retired to the back of the hall to listen. Hawk started to play 'Moonglow'—and it was harrowing in its awfulness. But gradually, the strength and the confidence returned, and after sixteen bars the great, majestic Hawkins sound was booming through the auditorium. Hawk did three numbers with Ben and played magnificently—making it purely on guts and instinct. It was an act of immense courage.

After the performance Hawk was rushed back to London and we called the Club doctor. Hawk was put to bed in his room at the Piccadilly Hotel, given a massive injection of antibiotics and told that any future playing engagements were out of the question for at least two weeks. But Hawkins wasn't about to let pneumonia disrupt his normal mode of life. As the doctor left he was sitting up in bed in his silk dressing gown, smoking a cigarette and, naturally, drinking a large goblet of Remy Martin with iced water on the side.

Hawkins was booked on a continental European tour which was due to begin in Stockholm the following day. The doctor told him quite emphatically that the journey would kill him. 'I'll be back in the morning to continue the treatment,' he said. But when he returned to the hotel early the next day, he found that Hawkins had checked out and had caught a plane for Stockholm. Apart from the pneumonia, Hawk had chronic bronchitis—but he completed the whole tour, sustained by various doctors and abundant quantities of Remy Martin along the way. However, even a man of his tremendous grit and spirit could not survive much longer the rigours of that gruelling routine, exacerbated by a diet of brandy and cigarettes. In May 1969, jazz lost the man who really introduced the tenor saxophone to jazz.

Archie Shepp, then the enfant terrible of the avant garde, was the second 'free' player to appear at the Club. His engagement preceded that of Hawkins and evoked very mixed reactions from the critics. Some of Shepp's output of that period has been described by Leonard Feather as 'anarchic, shrieking protest music' and it certainly did not make a favourable impression on everybody.

Our piano tuner, Alf Heckman, had been urging Pete King for months to allow him to sit through a rehearsal by a visiting American group. Alf, who was blind and used a guide dog, was a lover of melodic orthodox jazz and was very much hoping to have the chance of hearing a Bill Evans session or one by Blossom Dearie. But as luck would have it he came to tune the piano on the day that Archie Shepp's group was due to rehearse—and Pete invited him to stay on to listen. Shepp's band—with Roswell Rudd on trombone, Jimmy Garrison on bass and Beaver Harris on drums—assembled long before Heckman had finished tuning the piano and waited for him to complete the job. Alf finished, packed his bag, and moved towards a chair in front of the bandstand ready to sit down and listen. He was just lowering himself into the chair when the Shepp group cut loose with the most stridently discordant series of screams, whines, rattles, groans and agonised shrieks. Alf froze, half standing, half sitting, clearly unable to believe his ears as the din swelled to a raging, rampaging crescendo. Then he straightened up, shook his head sadly, and shuffled, mumbling, from the Club. He never asked to hear a rehearsal again.

I should emphasise that Archie Shepp and his cohorts were all excellent musicians, but at this particular time their music was somewhat difficult even for musically schooled people to assimilate. I remember Stan Getz and Coleman Hawkins sitting together in the Club through a particularly long, labyrinthine solo of honks, screeches and rasps by Shepp. After about ten minutes of this, Hawk turned to Getz and said straight-faced: 'Hey listen Stan—he's playing our tune.'

Veteran tenorist Bud Freeman made his début at the Club in 1967 as did Basie star Eddie 'Lockjaw' Davis and we had return visits from other superb exponents of my favourite instrument—Rollins, Lateef, Ben, Zoot (with Al Cohn) and Elvira 'Vi' Redd, a lady alto saxophonist from Los Angeles. In the vocal department we had Dakota Staton and the witty sophistication of Blossom Dearie. By now our booking agency, Ronnie Scott Directions, had become very active and we organised tours for both Blossom and Dakota.

The change of premises also brought about a change in the character of the audience. Whereas eighty-five per cent of the Gerrard Street audiences had been dedicated jazz enthusiasts, it dropped to around sixty-five per cent when we installed ourselves in Frith Street. But we did begin to get some star visitors. One night Miles Davis came into the Club with his entourage—including his dentist, hairdresser, lawyer and a couple of very impressive ladies—and we got a big kick out of that because Miles, a man of tremendous charisma, is one of those rare and aloof members of the jazz hierarchy who is held in considerable awe by jazz lovers and jazz musicians alike.

101

There was much deferential bowing and scraping, much fluttering of waitresses and a constant hiss of stage whispers as customers pointed out the great man to one another.

Miles, a slim, elegantly dressed figure with outsize dark glasses, sat through it all inscrutably. It was a momentous occasion—but it made no impression at all on Gypsy Larry, our general factotum. If he knew who Miles Davis was, he certainly didn't care—and when 3.30 am came and Miles and his party were still sitting at their tables, Larry appeared with his broom and unceremoniously turned them out. 'Come on, you lot—time to get out. I've got to sweep up here—come on, out of it'—and Miles and his acolytes got to their feet humbly and drifted quietly away into the night.

Larry went in awe of nobody at all—and neither did the American offbeat comedian, Professor Irwin Corey, whom we booked into the Club on one occasion. Miles Davis, who is an outspoken champion of the black people and has rather bitter views on their exploitation by the whites, again visited the Club with a large entourage and sat at a table right in front of the bandstand. In the middle of his act, Corey bent down and, with reckless intrepidity, snatched away Miles's enormous dark glasses. Corey then put them on, looked around the Club briefly, and said to Miles, 'Hey, no wonder you're smiling—everybody looks black.' Miles took it very well.

One of the first attractions of 1968 was the trio of one of the most influential drummers in modern jazz, Kenny Clarke, who had been resident in Paris since 1956 after having worked in the States with all the modern jazz giants. Then, after a return visit from Johnny Griffin, came singer Jon Hendricks, a man with an exceptional talent for setting intelligent lyrics to standard jazz tunes.

To maintain the saxophone quota we had two excellent exponents, each making his first appearance in Britain—altoist Phil Woods and tenorist Hank Mobley. And in August my new eight-piece band—with Kenny Wheeler, Chris Pyne, Ray Warleigh, John Surman, Gordon Beck, Ron Mathewson and Tony Crombie—made its début at the Club.

We'd hardly begun to make a dent in the repayment of the loan from Harold Davidson when Pete and I decided to plunge even deeper into the red. The premises next door became available and we saw a wonderful opportunity not only to enlarge the jazz room itself but also to add an upstairs room for live entertainment and a downstairs bar. With more assistance from our good friend Harold Davison, we began putting the extension work in hand. We kept the Club open as long as we could while the initial work was undertaken, but on 14 September, after a four-week season by one of my favourite saxophonists, Joe Henderson, we closed the Club for a couple of weeks so that the extension work could be completed.

We reopened on Monday, 30 September with the Buddy Rich Orchestra. Alterations were more or less finished but, once again, a few refinements were missing. Buddy Rich announced during his opening set: 'This is the first time I've played on a building site.'

Our first plan for the upstairs room was to run it on Old Place lines and use it as a showcase for British jazz musicians. We presented a few jazz groups there, including John Surman's, but it really didn't take off. We had another non-starter idea to present comedy films there, but we were unable to get the co-operation of the distributors. So the place became a discotheque and we adopted a policy of presenting up-and-coming pop, rock,

103

reggae and soul groups. Some of the acts which played there in the early days were Arrival, Peter Sarstedt, Osibisa, Linda Hoyle and Affinity—who later graduated to the jazz room—Heat Wave, the Jam and Kilburn and the High Roads.

Despite the total lack of commercial success, Pete and I have always tried to provide as many working opportunities as possible for British jazzmen and when we changed the policy of the upstairs room we did our best to open up more possibilities for British musicians to play opposite, or with, visiting American stars. We also started Sunday sessions for British musicians and later made the Club available without fee on Sundays to a musicians' co-operative so that they could present their own concerts. But we continued to suffer regular attacks on the grounds that we discriminated against British jazz musicians. At one point I was provoked to write a letter to the *Melody Maker* pointing out that for every one American musician who had played in the Club, we had hired six British musicians. I also explained that keeping the Old Place open two years after we moved to Frith Street had cost us between £100 and £125 a week and had left us with a final debt of £3,000. I concluded that if British musicians wanted to find somewhere to play they should do what I did and open a club. 'The best thing,' I said, 'is to find a philanthropic, jazz-crazed millionaire. And if you do find one, please introduce him to me. I've been looking for one for years.'

The tenth anniversary year of the Club, 1969, saw a number of innovations including an appearance by the comedy group, the Scaffold and a double guitar bill featuring classical guitarist John Willimas and jazz guitarist Barney Kessel. The experiment worked extremely well and I was so captivated by the superb musicianship of John Williams that I was inspired to buy a Spanish guitar and start taking lessons. My great hope was to learn at least one simple guitar piece before I died. I took six lessons and after the last one the teacher said to me, earnestly, 'Do you have a job to fall back on, Mr Scott?' From that point on the guitar became a wall ornament. John Williams played several times at the Club—once opposite Soft Machine. Quite recently the celebrated flautist, James Galway, approached me and asked if we ever booked classical musicians. I told him about John Williams and he said, 'Well, would you like me to play down here?' I said I'd be delighted.

'Do you think I should work with just a piano, or with a string quartet?' he asked. I told him, as I began turning the pages of the engagement diary, that anything he felt like doing would be OK with us. 'Well, that's fine,' he said. 'You must talk to my agent about it. Mind you, it couldn't be until 1986. . .'

A much-acclaimed début at the Club in February 1969 was that of the magnificent multi-national big band which Kenny Clarke and Belgian pianist-composer-arranger Francy Boland co-led between 1962 and 1972. I had the honour of playing in that band, which was conceived, sustained and inspired by a dynamic Italian-born big band swing enthusiast, Gigi Campi, who financed his hobby from the profits he made from a highly successful café and icecream business in Cologne's famous Hohestrasse. Among the fine musicians who worked in that band were Johnny Griffin, Derek Humble, Sahib Shihab, Tony Coe, Benny Bailey, Idrees Sulieman, Ake Persson, Dusko Goykovich, Nat Peck and Ron Mathewson. It was a fantastic band while it lasted.

Another superb big band which made the first of several appearances that year at the Club was that of Thad Jones and Mel Lewis. We also presented the Johnny Dankworth Orchestra with Cleo Laine and Stan Getz made a return visit.

In August the Club was taken over for a couple of weeks by a BBC television crew for a special series of jazz programmes which were filmed for transmission later on BBC 2. A number of top musicians performed before an invited audience each night and we didn't open the Club to the public until about 10.30 pm. It was a very impressive line-up: Miles Davis (making his first and only appearance at the Club), Lionel Hampton, Sarah Vaughan, Cecil Taylor, the Oscar Peterson Trio, the Clarke-Boland Band and the Buddy Rich Orchestra. Terry Henebery, the producer of the programmes, asked me to act as compere for the series and this meant that on the final Sunday of the two-week schedule, I had to do about forty-five separate links to introduce all the different segments of the sixteen-week series, and I had to do it as though the whole thing was live. I remember that just before the cameras started rolling, Terry Henebery said, 'We'd better arrange a few changes of costume for you Ronnie as this is going to be spread over three or four months.'

'Don't worry,' I told him. 'I've got a suit for every day of the week. And this is it.'

One of the most memorable nights of that period was when Buddy Rich's Orchestra played. Buddy was in top wisecracking form and constantly sending the whole thing up. But he and the band obviously enjoyed their set so much that they agreed to do a free encore for the audience after the cameras had been switched off for the night. To this unexpected bonus was added the further plus of having Jon Hendricks and Annie Ross, who were in the audience, take the stage to sing with the band some of the brilliant repertoire from their days in the Lambert, Hendricks & Ross vocal group. It was a fantastic night and Buddy and the band excelled themselves.

People always used to tell us that Buddy Rich could be a tough man to deal with, but we've always got along well with him. Of course, he doesn't suffer fools gladly and if anyone in the audience is incautious enough to heckle him, then Buddy will rapidly cut him to pieces with a ferocious barrage of whiplash sarcasm. Buddy could earn a handsome living as a stand-up comedian and he constantly tosses out devastating ad-lib comments which any professional comic would be proud to steal. During one engagement at the Club, Buddy concluded his set, walked to the front of the stage and said, 'We'll be back later—meanwhile Ronnie Scott will be on to tell you the same old jokes.' So when the time came to introduce Buddy's next set, I just had to say: 'And in just a few moments Buddy Rich will be back to play you the same old drum solos.' He took it very well.

The spontaneous set by Jon Hendricks and Annie Ross was one of those unexpected moments on which jazz clubs thrive and it really is a pity that 'sitting-in' seems to have become something of a lost art. There used to be a good deal more of it at the Old Place—sometimes more than was really desirable. It was hard to control and you couldn't always guarantee that the sitter-in would be compatible with the band on stage. There was a time when organist Richard 'Groove' Holmes dealt with a determined and clearly juiced sitter-in by changing key every chorus until he'd gone through all twelve. But there were some superb spontaneous sessions—such as the night at the Old Place, during Annie Ross's gig, when Ella Fitzgerald and Mel Torme joined her on stage. Guitarist José Feliciano made a spontaneous guest appearance just before he became a major star and Jimi Hendrix sat in with Eric Burdon and War the night before he died. And when Zoot Sims was last at the Club, Phil Woods and Michel Legrand sat in with him. According to Phil, Zoot asked, 'What shall we play, Michel—'Cherokee'?' And Michel said, 'What about 'I Will Wait For You'? Then Phil said, 'How about 'Indiana'?.' And Michel said, 'Let's try 'Watch What Happens'.' 'We could do 'All The Things You Are',' said Zoot. 'Or 'What Are You Doing The Rest Of Your Life'?' suggested Legrand. I believe they finished up doing a Michel Legrand medley.

Interlude 10

Over the years we've had some very attractive waitresses working at the Club. We had one girl who looked like Barbarella. Sir John Barbarella.

Then we had a girl called Bonnie who came from Australia—which is a wonderful place. To come from.

Bonnie was very modest, I remember—she was so modest she used to eat bananas sideways.

Some of the girls are pretty but not very bright. I remember speaking to one waitress once about books and I asked her if she liked Dickens. She said she didn't know, she'd never been to one.

She also thought that Moby Dick was a venereal disease.

Another girl we had was very good looking. Before she came to us she'd been an air hostess. For the Wright Brothers.

Then we had a very nice little girl who came all the way from India. She flew here by Air Bombay and she told me something about that airline which I never knew before. It seems that they only serve meals to the first class passengers. But they let the tourist class passengers come up and beg.

Of course we get all classes of people in the Club—some of them very high class indeed. Which is why Jeff Ellison, who was on the door at the Frith Street Club for twelve years, used to say that he was a doorman to royalty.

Tenth Set:

___

The old routine

The first ten years were the hardest, yet the time seemed to pass amazingly rapidly—and the pace has accelerated ever since, so that the last ten years seem to have taken a fraction of that time to elapse. It would take far too long to list all the brilliant—and some not so brilliant—artists who paraded through the Club between 1969 and 1979—but these are some of major names we took pride in presenting:

1970—Charles Mingus, Stan Getz, Charlie Shavers, Earl Hines, Roland Kirk.

1971—Harry James, Maynard Ferguson, Herbie Mann, Anita O'Day.

1972—Stan Kenton, Bill Evans, Thad Jones-Mel Lewis, Chico Hamilton, the Modern Jazz Quartet, Stephane Grappelli, Chuck Mangione, Weather Report, Chick Corea, Back Door.

1973—Dizzy Gillespie, Oscar Peterson, Art Blakey's Jazz Messengers, George Melly for the first time (but not the last, God help us!), Buddy Rich, Alex Welsh, Jimmy Witherspoon, Freddie Hubbard and a return visit from Mangione.

1974—Woody Herman, Ella Fitzgerald, Sonny Rollins, Bill Evans, Elvin Jones, George Benson, Joe Pass, Oscar Peterson, Carmen McRae, Roland Kirk, Illinois Jacquet, Tom Scott, Junior Mance.

1975—Stan Kenton, Joe Pass, Clark Terry, Cecil Taylor, Milt Jackson, Roy Eldridge, Zoot Sims, Monty Alexander, the Count Basie Band.

1976—Cedar Walton, Frank Rosolino, Woody Herman, Oscar Peterson, Lee Konitz with Warne Marsh, Stan Getz, Dizzy Gillespie, Horace Silver, Milt Buckner, Carrie Smith, Betty Carter, Woody Shaw.

1977—Dexter Gordon, George Coleman with Tete Montoliu, Sarah Vaughan, Roy Eldridge, Joe Pass, Bobby Hutcherson, Dizzy Gillespie, Stan Getz, Horace Silver.

1978—Toots Thielemans, Dexter Gordon, Helen Humes, Freddie Hubbard, Mary Lou Williams, Art Blakey, John Williams, George Coleman, Earl Hines, Harry Edison with Eddie Lockjaw Davis.

1979—Cedar Walton, Carrie Smith, Johnny Griffin, Houston Person, Alex Welsh, Georgie Fame, Barbara Thompson, Elaine Delmar, Art Blakey, Dorothy Donegan, Scott Hamilton.

And aside from the long list of jazz artists we've presented at the Club, there are all kinds of jazz fringe entertainers whose appearances somehow tend to be forgotten—artists like Tom Waits, Jackie Cain and Roy Kral, Al Jarreau, Brand X, the Surprise Sisters, Mose Allison, the Four Freshmen, Jack Bruce, Elkie Brooks, Joan Armatrading, Linda Lewis, Maria Muldaur, Tanya Maria, Doris Troy, Esther Marrow, Esther Phillips, Viola Wills, Betty Davis.

Throughout the last ten years I have managed to keep my hand in as a practising musician and never seemed to have too much trouble in finding work. After the eight-piece band broke up I formed a trio with Mike Carr on organ and Tony Crombie (later Bobby Gien) on drums. We did gigs all over Britain and also played dates in

Hungary, France, Italy, Belgium, Portugal, Switzerland and Ireland. In 1972 I put together a big band to accompany Jack Jones on a British tour and re-formed the same band in 1973 to do some dates with Nancy Wilson.

The trio continued working until 1975 and made tours of Australia and the USA. We played a concert at Carnegie Hall and then had a week's engagement in Buddy Rich's Club in New York. Then in mid-1975 I formed a quintet with John Taylor on keyboards, Louis Stewart on guitar, Ron Mathewson on bass and Martin Drew on drums, and although there have been one or two changes in the piano department since, this quintet has proved to be one of the most satisfying bands I've ever had. We play an average of four gigs a week and I've been gratified by the revival jazz seems to be enjoying around the country. It is especially good to see the younger generation digging what we do.

The Quintet made its record début on the Ronnie Scott's Record Productions label which we launched in 1978 through Pye with additional albums by George Melly, Sarah Vaughan, Carmen McRae and Louis Stewart. The record label was something Pete and I had thought about for years in the interests of giving recording opportunities to some of the fine musicians, British and American, who appear at the Club.

The Quintet recording has its moments, but I genuinely hate listening to myself on record and I wouldn't care if I never made another album. My principal ambition is to be a better player—especially after having heard some of the greatest saxophone players in jazz at the Club. I suppose of all the great music I've heard there in the past twenty years, that produced by Rollins looms largest in my memory. It was also a thrill to hear the magnificent Basie Band in a club environment on the Count's one and only visit in

112

1975, and I'm proud of pulling of the considerable coup of being able to present the three leading ladies of jazz —Sarah Vaughan, Ella Fitzgerald and Carmen McRae. It has also been great to have in the Club such giants as Oscar Peterson and those two superlative, veteran sax-ophonists, Coleman Hawkins and Ben Webster. Then there's Buddy Rich, and Stan Getz and, of course, we have a special soft spot for Zoot Sims. I'm gratified to say that not one of the scores of fine jazz artists we have presented at the Club has disappointed. We've had one or two who weren't able to go on because they were smashed out of their minds, but, on the whole, the level of performance and professionalism has been outstanding. You hear a lot about jazz musicians being slaves to drugs and drink, but our doctor will tell you that of all the players who have worked at the Club, less than one per cent had a drug problem. 'There's a far higher incidence of drug addiction among doctors,' he says. And as for drink—well, musi-cians are no better and no worse than plumbers, police-men or pantechnicon drivers. In fact, many of the modern musicians are far too earnestly devoted to mastering their instruments to risk dulling their reflexes with drink or drugs.

One musician who was addicted still appears at the Club occasionally and he was at one time spending more than £40,000 dollars a year on heroin. Nowadays he has all the puritanical zeal of the reformed prostitute. Not long ago our doctor took him and his wife out for a meal to celebrate his kicking the habit and he found that the musician, who as an addict had been an extremely witty and entertaining speaker, had been transformed by his cure into a boring, pedantic and impossibly smug pain in the neck. 'This sort of thing is not uncommon,' the doctor tells me. 'People

113

who have been slaves to a habit for years and then, through a tremendous effort of will conquer the craving, often become sanctimonious proselytisers. It is just like a man who has been a confirmed atheist for years suddenly developing a fanatical evangelical fervour.'

Of the small number of musicians the Club doctor has treated for addiction, one, a visiting drummer, baffled him completely. The man was having wild hallucinations and practically foaming at the mouth and the doctor kept urging him to say what kind of drug he had been using so that he could prescribe something safe to ease the symptons and bring the poor guy out of his wildly disturbed state. Time and again the doctor asked the question, but drummer stubbornly refused to answer. At length, after an infinite amount of perseverance and persuasion, the doctor managed to elicit from the musician the fact that he had kicked his habit years ago but had swapped it for what, it seemed, was an equally enslaving and mind-blowing addiction to a religious cult whose leader apparently had the power to send him from time to time into a state bordering on convulsive epilepsy.

What has presented far more of a problem than drugs for some of our visitors has been the exemplary vigilance of the Inland Revenue. Musicians tend to be a little careless about such things as tax returns. They collect their money after an engagement, neglect to declare their earnings to the tax authorities and the next time they arrive at Heathrow they are likely to be buttonholed by men bearing buff envelopes. It happened with Johnny Griffin in 1969 when he arrived to join the Clarke-Boland Band for its first engagement at the Club. Johnny had assumed that tax had been deducted from his money when he had worked for us before—but he was in error. The band had

114

just completed a rehearsal at the Club on the afternoon of the Monday they were due to open. It was about 7 pm. Johnny was getting ready to head back to his hotel when he was told that three men had arrived to see him. The men had a warrant for his arrest for contempt of court. This was a major disaster because Johnny was a vital member of the band. We all went into the office and tried to make contact with the judge who had signed the court order so that we could tell him it was all a mistake. But the judge was out somewhere getting sober. So then we tried getting the officials to call their wives and bring them to the Club for an evening 'on the house'—but that didn't wash.

'Why can't you let him play and take him to jail after the Club closes?' I asked.

'Hey,' Johnny cried, in a wounded tone. 'I'm not going to play for you guys and then be carted off to jail. You're only thinking of the band. What about me? I'm going to escape—if you cats want me to play you're gonna have to handcuff me to the music desk.'

We couldn't budge the heavies so Johnny was taken off to jail and he spent the next eighteen hours in Pentonville, purging his contempt. I think he had to pay a £200 fine on top of the tax due in the end—and I hear he pays his taxes pretty promptly these days. Johnny and I were talking about that episode recently and he said to me: 'If anybody at Pentoville reads your book, I gotta tell them that they must change that fish soup. Jesus Christ, I've never tasted anything so horrible in my life!'

Another man to have tax problems was the late Charles Mingus, one of the great bassists in jazz, a prolific and distinctive composer who had something of a provocative and combative personality. When he made his début at the

115

Club in 1971, he was rapidly tracked down by the Inland Revenue who wanted to collect some tax from him on the fees he was paid for taking part in the 1961 British movie 'All Night Long', together with Dave Brubeck, John Dankworth, Tubby Hayes and a few other jazzmen. Mingus, a towering, formidable figure, was just about to start his set one night when a timorous little African in a pin-stripped suit appeared and, with immense trepidation, explained that he had to serve him a writ. Word of Mingus's explosive temper had obviously filtered through to the Inland Revenue officials who presumably had considered it a master stroke to confront the bassist with a fellow black. Mingus seemed ready to erupt but Pete King pacified him and explained the procedure: 'Just take the paper, Charles—you have to be seen to receive it—then you can hand it to me and we'll get the Club lawyer to sort it out.'

Mingus took the writ and glared malevolently at the fast-retreating figure of the little African. For the next five minutes Mingus stood motionless and taciturn, laboriously reading every word on the writ. Then he strode on to the stage, waved the writ at the audience and roared with bloodcurdling venom: 'I've just had a letter from your Queen!' He seized his bass and for the next ten minutes hammered all kinds of indignant hell out of it.

Since we moved from our Gerrard Street cellar to the more comfortable and presentable premises in Frith Street, we have had quite a number of celebrity guests. Marlon Brando—a keen amateur bongoes player—was in regularly, while he was making a film here, to see Mongo Santamaria. He and Gypsy Larry got on famously together. Spike Milligan and John Le Mesurier have been regular visitors and Jeff Ellison, our former doorman,

116

reckons that we once had a visit from a Pamela Motown, whom he thought, was connected in some way with Stevie Wonder. It was also Jeff who confronted singer Jack Jones at the door when he arrived with a friend one evening and told him: 'You can come in free, Mr Jones, but your friend will have to pay.' The friend was Tony Bennett.

We had fairly hilarious visit once from Adam West, the actor who plays Batman. He got into a somewhat overtired state and developed a sudden infatuation for one of our waitresses. She didn't respond at all enthusiastically to his overtures so Batman followed her all over the Club, upstairs into the disco, downstairs into the bar, trying to evoke a more friendly response. 'I'm Batman,' he kept saying to her. 'You know—Batman?'

It was when he was negotiating the stairs down from the discotheque in hot pursuit of the girl that he lost his footing and plunged, base over apex, to the bottom, landing in an inert and unconscious heap by the sound box.

Jeff on the door ran across to help him and not knowing the guy's real name said, 'Hey, Batman, wake up!' But Batman was out cold. So Jeff changed his tack; looked around the Club and yelled, 'Robin, come quick! It's Batman!' This was taken up gleefully by the staff and then by some of the customers until everyone in the Club seemed to be calling for Robin. Poor Batman eventually came to and limped silently away.

We've had Robert Wagner in the Club, Danny LaRue, Clive Jenkins, Lee Marvin and the Hon Gerald Lascelles—thought not all at the same table. But we haven't yet had the Dagenham Girl Pipers, Charles Manson, Max Bygraves, Terry Wogan, Des O'Connor and Enoch Powell—although I keep announcing them, hopefully, every week.

It is no secret that of our most distinguished guests has been Princess Margaret who has visited the Club on three or four occasions. Usually someone phones from the Palace to say she'll be along and can we reserve a table for her party. The last time she came was to see Oscar Peterson. She also saw Roland Kirk on one of his appearances at the Club. She came in with film director Bryan Forbes and his wife, and Peter Sellers. I told Roland the Princess was in the Club but added that on no account should he make any reference to her presence. Discretion was essential, I said. I should have realised that discretion was anathema to Roland. As soon as he took the stand he roared into the microphone: 'We'd like thank all the beautiful people who've come in to see us tonight—Peter Sellers, Bryan Forbes, Nanette Newman and Princess Margaret.' That was bad enough, but Spike Milligan capped it comprehensively on another occasion when Princess Margaret came to the Club, and nearly had me banished to the Tower. Spike was supposed to be joining the Princess, Peter Sellers and another couple at the Club that night but for some reason was unable to make it. He telephoned me in the late afternoon and said that he had wanted to send a telegram to Peter Sellers apologising for his absence but it was now too late. Therefore he was going to get me to take down a message and wanted me to read it out at the Club that night as though it were a telegram.

The Princess and her party arrived at about 11 pm and as soon as the set that was in progress ended, I went on stage, took the mike and said, 'I have just received a telegram from Spike Milligan addressed to Peter Sellers and it runs as follows:

'Wherever you are, wherever you be,
Please take your hand off the Princess's knee'

Later, as I was passing her table, she looked up at me and said with a rather frosty smile, 'I liked your joke.'

'Oh, it wasn't mine,' I said hastily , 'that was Mr Milligan's'.

The incident was all over the papers the next day and there were some very pompous comments about Spike abusing his relationship with the Royal Family by resorting to cheap jokes. But it was all very harmless.

Spike is a great jazz fan and he takes the music very seriously. Whenever he comes to the Club he invariably complains about the high conversation level. He keeps asking me to instal a pair of earphones near his favourite table so that he can listen to the music direct through the sound system and not be bothered by the babble of conversation. The funny thing is, though, that he is often one of the noisiest members of the audience. One of these days when he telephones and asks to be given a table away from the chatter, I'm going to have to tell him, 'Look, Spike, wherever we seat you, you're going to be near Milligan.'

Spike has a great line in offbeat comedy and, as anyone who has visited the Club in the last fourteen or fifteen years knows, I have a special liking for oblique humour. I began doing a regular, between-sets routine soon after we moved into Frith Street. I think you have to have some kind of a sense of humour to be a jazz musician, otherwise you'd go potty sitting in band coaches and trains for hours on end.

Ever since I was very young I knocked around with guys who had a sharp sense of humour and I guess some of it rubbed off. I've built up my routine over the years picking up one-liners here and there. I suppose I've always thought that injecting humour into the proceedings would keep things from being on too ponderous a level. Most of

119

the comedians I like are American—Lennie Bruce, Bob Newhart, Woody Allen, Don Rickles, Jackie Mason, Henny Youngman—and Rodney Dangerfield is a fantastic comic. I think there are good English comics like Ronnie Barker, John Cleese, Spike Milligan and Max Wall, but the one-liner is strictly an American institution.

I know the routine I do is constantly criticised for parading the same old jokes, but I slip a new one in from time to time. Someone recently played me a tape of a routine I did about ten years ago and I realised that there were a lot of jokes I hadn't been using for years. So I'm giving them the kiss of life and putting them back in the act. I know that many of the people who come to the Club have heard the jokes dozens of times before, but there are always people to whom they are new. And I actually get requests for jokes now—'Tell the one about chemist . . .' they say. I think it is nice to leaven the music with a little humour—even if we do often get a party of dead Greeks at the front table who remain totally impervious to everything I say. Anyway I reckon I can keep the routine going for at least another twenty years.

I can't finish this self-indulgent catalogue of personal recollection without paying tribute to all the people who have helped make it possible—the hundreds of fine musicians and singers, the paying and non-paying customers, the reviewers, the critics, the agents, the bookers, artist managers, recording companies, promoters—all the thousands of people here and abroad who have been involved, directly or indirectly, in helping to make Ronnie Scott's Club exactly the kind of place Pete and I always hoped it would be.

I also want to acknowledge the debt Pete and I owe to all the people who have worked for us over the last twenty years—Joe the chef, Arthur, Gypsy Larry, Alex, Roy the head waiter, Jeff Ellison, Henry Cohen, Roxy Beaujolais (Jenny Hoffmann), Brian Theobald, Chips Chipperfield, Jimmy Parsons, Martin Lyder, George Clarke, Nina, Keith McDonald—and all the others whose loyalty has helped make the job that much easier. I'd just like to leave them with one question: 'Where are you all working next week?'

Special thanks to Harold Davison for his generous support when we needed it most; and, most of all, thanks to my friend and partner Pete King, who has always done a good job. Very badly. . . . Just kidding!

But don't think it hasn't all been worthwhile. Because it hasn't. It's made a happy man very old.

Finally, if we don't see you at the Club next week, have a good week. And if we never see you again, have a good life.

Interlude 11

And now, before Spike Milligan appears for the final set, I want you to know that our waiters and waitresses will be very pleased to take you. Er, to take care *of you.*

And Martin, our maitre d', *will see that you are comfortably seated. Martin is also our sound man—the greatest sound man in the country. In the city . . . useless.*

Actually Martin comes from Germany. He used to be in show business there during the war and had a very big following. Storm troopers, mostly.

Martin recently had a hair transplant. They took the hair from under his arms and put it on his head. And it looks great.

But it stinks.

He goes to a lot of trouble to keep looking young—hormone

injections, plastic surgery. All a waste of money. There's only one way to keep looking young—hang around with old people.

Martin's a very well-educated guy, though. He took medicine at Oxford. Feels much better now.

He once wrote a letter of complaint to the Tampax company, saying: 'I've been using your product for six months. Still can't swim, play tennis or ride a bike.'

Well, so much for humour—and now, in just a few moments, Spike Milligan. . . .

Coda:

All that Jewish jazz
Spike Milligan

Lying in bed in Johannesburg hospital with tick bite fever is, of course, an ideal time to be asked to write a postscript to this book. The requests were as follows: (1) Why I like going to Ronnie Scott's Jazz Club, and (2) Something personal about Ronnie.

All right: I love his jazz Club. I hate the noisy bloody customers, who sometimes speak so loud that you would think it was part of the musical arrangement that's going on on the stand. I myself, sitting in a dark corner, often burst into a Schubert aria, to add to the confusion, and nobody seems to notice the difference. However I will say this, he does try to employ first class, world class jazz musicians, and sometimes when all the oafs haven't come in to hear themselves eat, there are quiet occasions with Stephane Grappelli and John Williams. As he says, I did once ask him if he could run a pair of earphones to my table, so I could plug directly into the sound system to exclude the vociferous homendus and early Javanese ape men. Alas he never complied, and in this paragraph he has to pay the penalty. The waitresses are obliging and the food tolerable and if you point a loaded pistol at the waiter he will give you an ice bucket.

Now to Ronnie himself, whom I must admit I prefer very much to the Club. First he is a consummate musician. He is possibly one of the world's most articulate and

123

creative tenor sax players. He has the range to be witty, morose, moody and sometimes Jewish in his playing. This is remarkable in that most musicians in America who have turned to running clubs have dropped out of the playing, and just become managers. Not so with Scott. In fact, whenever I see his group billed as the House Band, more often than not, he outshines the stars he has booked to play. If jazz had not gone so lamentably out of fashion with the coming of pop, he would possibly be an extremely wealthy man today. (I am sure he can't be extremely wealthy with those suits he wears.)

Indeed I can't praise him highly enough as a musician who plays with that rare ingredient, musical intellect rather than emotion; and I praise him in the all the years I have known him for never having finished his act with 'My Yiddisha Mama', a great rarity for a member of the Hebrew race. I suspect Ronnie has a suspicion I am a Nazi, because whenever I enter the Club he immediately tries to keep me quiet by sending a bottle of Mateus rosé to my table.

Now we come to his unexpected talent, of being a very funny stand-up comic. He delivers lines with all the vitriolic drive we have in George Burns, W. C. Fields and Groucho Marx. Even though I have heard his jokes many, many times (some of them I originated myself) he still manages to convulse me with laughter. He handles a late night, semi-drunk audience almost as if they were in kindergarten. I suppose in this respect he must be one of the few unique musicians in the world who successfully combines music and comedy with professional skill; the only other one I know is Buddy Rich. So it's timely that Ronnie should write a book about himself and the Club. He is one of the characters of London and one of the characters of music. But for him there would be no real venue to hear consistently good jazz, provided you have good hearing that is. A word of warning; if you should come out of the Club late at night, you will see sitting on the pavement, a broken-down figure in an old Army overcoat with a cap pulled down over the face, holding out a begging bowl, with a card saying, 'World War II Hero, Give Generously'. Don't be fooled, that is Ronnie Scott too; he insists on cashing in right up to the last minute.

And if I don't get a free book, this postscript is null and void.